AMOS, HOSEA, AND MICAH

CASCADE COMPANIONS

The Christian theological tradition provides an embarrassment of riches: from Scripture to modern scholarship, we are blessed with a vast and complex theological inheritance. And yet this feast of traditional riches is too frequently inaccessible to the general reader.

The Cascade Companions series addresses the challenge by publishing books that combine academic rigor with broad appeal and readability. They aim to introduce nonspecialist readers to that vital storehouse of authors, documents, themes, histories, arguments, and movements that comprise this heritage with brief yet compelling volumes.

RECENT TITLES IN THIS SERIES:

AMOS, HOSEA, AND MICAH

Hebrew Prophets of the Eighth Century

JACK R. LUNDBOM

 CASCADE *Books* · Eugene, Oregon

AMOS, HOSEA, AND MICAH
Hebrew Prophets of the Eighth Century

Cascade Companions

Cascade Books
An Imprint of Wipf and Stock Publishers
199 W. 8th Ave., Suite 3
Eugene, OR 97401

www.wipfandstock.com

PAPERBACK ISBN: 978-1-5326-5635-4
HARDCOVER ISBN: 978-1-5326-5636-1
EBOOK ISBN: 978-1-5626-5637-8

Cataloguing-in-Publication data:

Name: Lundbom, Jack R., author.

Title: Amos, Hosea, and Micah : Hebrew prophets of the eighth
century / Jack R. Lundbom.

Description: Eugene, OR: Cascade Books, 2021. | Cascade
Companions. | Includes bibliographical references and indexes.

Identifiers: ISBN: 978–1-5326–5635–4 (paperback). | ISBN: 978-1-
5326-5636-1 (hardcover). | ISBN: 978-1-5626-5637-8 (ebook).

Subjects: LSCH: Bible. Minor Prophets—Criticism, interpretation,
etc. | Amos—Criticism, interpretation, etc. | Hosea—Criticism,
interpretation, etc. | Micah—Criticism, interpretation, etc.

Classification: BS1560.A3 L86 2021 (print). | BS1560.A3 (ebook).

To
Bohdan Hroban
Educator, Scholar, Churchman

CONTENTS

Contents

PREFACE

THIS BOOK SEEKS TO put before general readers background and selected preaching of three Hebrew prophets in the eighth century: Amos, Hosea, and Micah. In line with other books in the Cascade Companions series it limits technical discussion and footnotes, leaving readers to consult larger commentaries and selected works cited in the bibliography. Passages chosen are some of the most familiar from each prophet and some of the most important, dealing with faithfulness, justice and righteousness, a broken covenant between Israel and its God, and after judgment the hope for a surviving remnant. God's moral governance of the whole world is also to be seen in Amos. In the discussion questions I have attempted to make connections to teachings in the New Testament and to issues arising in today's world.

Some words of these prophets will be difficult to hear. Criticism is never easy to hear, especially strong criticism. But it must be remembered that Scripture reveals a great God who loves justice and righteousness, faithfulness and steadfast love, and is benevolent to the poor and needy. Israel, too, at its best, carried out these lofty principles, in part because later if not earlier it countenanced prophets who cried out loudly when they were not being carried out. Americans would do well to keep the same in mind as we seek to live out high principles as a nation, accepting needed criticism later if not earlier.

I am dedicating this book to my good friend Dr. Bohdan Hroban, president of the Center for Christian Education in Martin, Slovakia. Besides being an innovative director of this fine Lutheran school in postcommunist Slovakia, Bohdan is an excellent scholar and a respected churchman. His scholarly work has focused on Isaiah and the Psalms.

Jack R. Lundbom
Kennebunk, Maine
January 1, 2021

ABBREVIATIONS

ABD	*Anchor Bible Dictionary*, edited by David Noel Freedman. 6 vols. New York: Doubleday, 1992
ANE	Ancient Near East
*ANET*³	*Ancient Near Eastern Texts Relating to the Old Testament*. Edited by James B. Pritchard. 3rd ed. with Supplement. Princeton: Princeton University Press, 1969
Ant.	*Antiquities of the Jews* (Josephus)
ArBib	The Aramaic Bible
CBSC	Cambridge Bible for Schools and Colleges
JB	Jerusalem Bible
JBC	*Jerome Biblical Commentary*. Edited by Raymond E. Brown et al. 2 vols. in 1. Englewood Cliffs, NJ: Prentice-Hall, 1968
JSS	*Journal of Semitic Studies*
KJV	King James Version
LXX	The Greek Septuagint of the Hebrew Bible / Old Testament

Abbreviations

m.	Mishnah
NEA	*Near Eastern Archaeology*
NT	New Testament
NCB	New Century Bible
NRSV	New Revised Standard Version of the Bible
OT	Old Testament
r.	reigned
RSV	Revised Standard Version of the Bible
VT	*Vetus Testamentum*

1

ISRAEL AND JUDAH IN THE EIGHTH CENTURY

IN THE EIGHTH CENTURY Israel was a divided nation; it had been so since the death of Solomon in 922 BC, when northerners under Jeroboam I pulled out of the union after Rehoboam, Solomon's son, rebuffed them at Shechem (1 Kgs 12:1–20). The ten tribes living north of Jerusalem and in Transjordan retained the name Israel. Jeroboam became king of the Northern Kingdom. The remaining tribe in the south was Judah (Simeon was absorbed soon after the Conquest), and Rehoboam reigned over Judah in Jerusalem.

Amos and Hosea, perhaps also Micah, preached in the mid-eighth century, a time that brought prosperity to both Israel and Judah. This was due largely to two very able kings, Jeroboam II in the north (r. 786–746 BC), and Uzziah (Azariah) in the south (r. 783–742 BC). Both states reached their zenith during the reigns of these kings. For Israel, the menace of Syria ended with the Assyrian destruction of

Damascus circa 802 BC. Egypt was in decline, and Assyria was no longer making incursions into the country or taking tribute from Samaria, largely because of internal dissention and a series of ineffectual rulers. Jeroboam by 760 was able to take Damascus and extend his northern boundary to the entrance of Hamath and also to recover Transjordanian territory lost by Jehu (r. 842–815 BC). When Jeroboam recovered Transjordan (2 Kgs 14:23–25; Amos 6:13) he extended its southern boundary to the Sea of the Arabah (the Dead Sea), thus gaining control of the King's Highway, the major trade route in the region. This brought him great wealth, as it had for Solomon earlier. Jeroboam was aided in his expansionist policy by Jonah ben Imittai, a prophet given only passing mention by the Deuteronomic Historian (2 Kgs 14:25), but one who later gained fame in a fictional work (the book of Jonah) portraying him as an unwilling preacher of judgment against a foreign nation.

In Judah, Uzziah (Azariah) ended a period of weakness by repairing the defenses of Jerusalem, reorganizing the army, and carrying on an expansionist policy of his own. He took tribute from the Ammonites and gained control over Edom. He also rebuilt the port at Ezion-geber (Elath) and restored trade routes into northern Arabia. Uzziah had complete control of the Negeb and the southern desert, and in the west retook the Philistine cities of Gath, Jabneh, and Ashdod (2 Kgs 14:22; 2 Chr 26:2, 6–15). Later in his reign he was struck with scale disease (2 Kgs 15:5), but nevertheless seems to have remained in control after his son Jotham began a co-reign and took over duties of state circa 750. So by the mid-eighth century, the boundaries of Israel and Judah were about what they were under Solomon, and prosperity of the Solomonic era returned. The two kings were also at peace with each other, which made for political stability in both north and south. But each nation was in an advanced state of decay, socially, morally, and religiously. It was especially so in Israel.

Things changed quickly when Tiglath-pileser III ascended the Assyrian throne in 745 BC, a year after Jeroboam died. In less than twenty-five years Israel would cease to exist. Beginning in 743, Tiglath-pileser made a number of campaigns into Syria and the coastal areas of Palestine, and by 738 was taking tribute from most states in Syria, Phoenicia, and northern Palestine, including Hamath, Tyre, Byblos, Damascus, and Samaria. This new Assyrian ruler (r. 745–727 BC) came west with the intent to conquer and occupy, and he was not to be denied.

Israel in the ensuing period experienced anarchy in the capital city and was unblessed by a series of inept rulers (2 Kgs 15:8–28). Israel had five kings in the ten years following Jeroboam's death. Jeroboam's son Zechariah was murdered after reigning six months by Shallum ben Jabesh, who was in turn liquidated in one month by Menahem ben Gadi. Israel was in a civil war. Menahem (r. 745–738 BC) ruled three years, being succeeded by his son Pekahiah (r. 738–737 BC), who was assassinated by one of his officers, Pekah ben Remaliah, who then took the throne. Pekah reigned for five years (737–732 BC).

During his reign Tiglath-pileser overran Galilee and Transjordan and took exiles to Assyria (2 Kgs 15:29). Megiddo and Hazor were destroyed. Pekah was then murdered by Hoshea ben Elah (2 Kgs 15:30), who surrendered to the Assyrians and gave tribute. In 732 Tiglath-pileser took Damascus. Hoshea ruled as an Assyrian vassal from 732 to 724. Shalmaneser V (r. 726–722 BC) succeeded Tiglath-pileser in 726, and Hoshea withheld tribute. In 724 his successor Shalmaneser V attacked and occupied what remained of Northern Israel, taking all but Samaria, which held out for about three years. Hoshea was taken prisoner.

In 722 Sargon II (r. 721–705 BC), who seized the throne after Shalmaneser's death, boasts of having conquered Samaria. But Shalmaneser may have taken the city (2 Kgs 17:1–6). Sargon deported a large portion of the population to Mesopotamia and Media (2 Kgs 17:5–6). Statehood for Northern Israel had ended.

Uzziah in the south died in 742 BC, but Judah managed to escape the disaster of the north due to the submission of King Ahaz (r. 735–715 BC) to Tiglath-pileser (2 Kgs 16:7–8). Judah was now beholden to its Assyrian overlord, and for all practical purposes had become a vassal state within the Assyrian Empire. It lost control of Edom and the port at Ezion-geber, and was economically weakened due to tribute demanded by the Assyrian king (2 Kgs 16:8, 17). There was also social and moral decay in Judah, like what brought ruin to Israel, though not on as great a scale. Ahaz's reign was remembered as one of great religious apostasy, with all sorts of pagan practices flourishing (2 Kgs 16:1–18).

The prophet Isaiah withdrew from public life after being rebuffed by Ahaz in 735 BC (Isa 8:16–18), and was not seen until twenty years later when Hezekiah became king. Micah may have begun his ministry about the same time as Isaiah, but we are unable to convincingly correlate his strident preaching with the reign of Ahaz. He did announce the destruction of Samaria but emerges into clear view only during Hezekiah's reign. Judah's day of reckoning would come at the hands of another Assyrian ruler, Sennacherib (r. 704–681), when it too would nearly come to an end. It survived, but just barely. In 701 Sennacherib reports in his Annals that he came into Judah and destroyed forty-six Judahite cities and countless small villages, leaving Hezekiah in Jerusalem "like a bird in a cage" (*ANET³*, 287–88).

This is confirmed by the biblical record (2 Kgs 18:13–16; Isa 1:4–9).[1]

Prophets in Jerusalem during the late eighth century were Micah and Isaiah, and possibly Hosea, who, according to the superscription of his book (Hos 1:1), is said to have been active during the reigns of Uzziah, Jotham (742–735 BC), Ahaz (735–715 BC), and Hezekiah (715–687/6 BC). This would seem to indicate that he came south after the destruction of Samaria, and could imply a later ministry overlapping with that of Micah and Isaiah. But of this nothing is known.

Hezekiah at the beginning of his reign sought to reverse policies of Ahaz, and had moderate success doing so. He removed the high places (2 Kings 16), centralized worship in Jerusalem, and was able to undertake a reform (2 Kgs 18:4, 22 = Isa 36:7; 2 Chr 29–31), which is best dated between 712 and 701 BC.[2] During the years 712–705 Sargon made no further campaigns into Palestine. Micah's dire prophecy against Zion was therefore averted, as we learn from later testimony at the trial of Jeremiah (Jer 26:17–19).

REFLECTION

1. Do we need to be especially vigilant when living in a prosperous time, when our nation is strong, wealthy, and nationalistic sentiments are strong?

2. How important is peace when the nation is in an advanced state of decay, socially, morally, and religiously?

---

1. On the theory of two campaigns by Sennacherib against Jerusalem, the latter being when the city was miraculously saved (2 Kgs 18:17—19:37; 2 Chr 32:1–23), see Lundbom, *Deuteronomy*, 445.

2. Lundbom, *Deuteronomy*, 442–46.

3. Isaiah was the great prophet of peace. Explain this against the background of the Assyrian invasion of Judah.

4. What is your assessment of the prophet Jonah who lived in North Israel and prophesied during the reign of Jeroboam II? Compare his message with the messages of Amos and Hosea.

2

AMOS, HOSEA, AND MICAH

THE TWELVE PROPHETS

AMOS, HOSEA, AND MICAH were three of the "Twelve Prophets" referred to in Sir 49:10, which says that they comforted the people of Jacob and gave them a confident hope. This group consists of Hosea, Joel, Amos, Obadiah, Jonah, Micah, Nahum, Habakkuk, Zephaniah, Haggai, Zechariah, and Malachi. Their prophecies were possibly contained on a separate scroll at the time Sirach was written, i.e., circa 180 BC. The collection has also been called the Minor Prophets, a title that seems first to have appeared in Augustine (*City of God* xviii, 29).[1] Augustine referred to the small size of the books when compared with the books of Isaiah, Jeremiah, and Ezekiel, which have come to be known collectively as the Major Prophets. The major prophet of the late eighth

1. Eissfeldt, *The Old Testament*, 383.

century was Isaiah, who is credited with most of chapters 1–39 in the book bearing his name.

WHAT MANNER OF INDIVIDUAL IS THE PROPHET?

The question was posed by Abraham Heschel, who said:

> Instead of showing us a way through the elegant mansions of the mind, the prophets take us to the slums. The world is a proud place, full of beauty, but the prophets are scandalized, and rave as if the whole world were a slum. They make much ado about paltry things, lavishing excessive language upon trifling subjects. What if somewhere in ancient Palestine poor people have not been treated properly by the rich? So what if some old women found pleasure and edification in worshiping "the Queen of Heaven"? Why such immoderate excitement? Why such intense indignation?[2]

Heschel goes on to say that things horrifying the prophets even now are daily occurrences all over the world. There is no society to which Amos's words in 8:4–6—about greedy merchants wanting the holidays to be over so they might trample the needy and poor with deceitful measures and false balances—would not apply. Heschel continues:

> Had a poet come to Samaria, the capital of the Northern Kingdom, he would have written songs exalting its magnificent edifices, its beautiful temples and worldly monuments. But when Amos of Tekoa came to Samaria, he spoke not of magnificence of palaces, but of moral confusion and oppression. Dismay filled the prophet:

2. Heschel, *The Prophets*, 3.

"I abhor the pride of Jacob, and hate his palaces,"
he cried out in the name of the Lord (Amos
6:8).[3]

DEUTERONOMY AND THE PROPHETS

The book of Deuteronomy is now thought to derive from
the late eighth or early seventh century, and many earlier scholars thought it originated among heirs to the great
eighth-century prophets. This would certainly include
Amos and Hosea, possibly also Micah and Isaiah. A century later things were reversed; now it was Deuteronomy
influencing the prophet Jeremiah.[4]

Amos

Amos came from Tekoa (1:1), a fortified town in the Ju-
dean highlands (2 Chr 11:5–6), now identified with Khir-
bet Tequ'a, roughly ten miles south of Jerusalem. It lay east
of the road from Bethlehem to Hebron. The site is three
thousand feet above sea level, on the border between ar-
able land and the desert. To the east was "the wilderness of
Tekoa" (2 Chr 20:20), otherwise known as "the wilderness
of Judea" (cf. Matt 3:1), which descended into the Dead Sea.
To the west was fertile land known for its olive trees (*m.
Menah* 8.3). There are ruins of a Byzantine church on the
site. The book bearing the prophet's name contains oracles
and reported visions, supplemented by a small amount of
biographical information (1:1; 7:10–15) and editorial com-
ment emanating from a different hand (3:1, 12; 5:1, 25–27;
6:9–10). Hopeful prophecy at the end (9:8c–15), what
Wellhausen called "roses and lavender instead of blood

3. Heschel, *The Prophets*, 8.

4. Lundbom, *Deuteronomy*, 28–43.

and iron,"[5] may well be an add-on by a later Judahite scribe. Amos considers the possibility of Yahweh being gracious to a "remnant of Joseph" (Amos 5:15), but one is left wondering if he will be. Amos's prophecies are otherwise unmitigated judgment. The idea of a surviving remnant of Israel began in earnest with Micah and Isaiah in the south.

Amos was among the shepherds of Tekoa. The Hebrew word for "shepherd" is not the usual one in the OT, occurring elsewhere only in 2 Kgs 3:4 where it is applied to Mesha, king of Moab. The term appears to mean "sheep master" or "sheep owner." He may also have been a "sheep breeder." Amos perhaps owned sheep, goats, and cattle, in which case he could have been a man of some means. In his response to the priest at Bethel Amos says he is also a "dresser of sycamore trees" (7:14). There is some amazing rhetoric and wisdom in Amos, and we may wonder where he got it. It was probably not at a school in Jerusalem, for we learn from the OT and other sources that wisdom thrives in desert tribes and in scarcely populated areas. For example, Job was from Uz in northwest in Arabia (Job 1:1), and his friend Eliphaz was a Temanite (Job 2:11; 4:1). Teman was a district in northeast Edom known for its wisdom (Jer 49:7).

The superscription to his book says that Amos preached during the reigns of Uzziah, king of Judah, and Jeroboam son of Joash, king of Israel. His preaching is usually dated after Jeroboam's victory over Damascus, probably circa 750 BC, although some date it a decade or so before 750, which is when Uzziah's co-regency with Jotham began (Jotham goes unmentioned in 1:1). Lo-debar and Karnaim in Gilead were recaptured at this time (6:13–14). It would also correlate with the earthquake mentioned in 1:1, which is dated circa 760. Hosea's appearance in the north is usually dated just after Amos began preaching.

5. Wellhausen, *Die kleinen Propheten*, 96.

The superscription states that Amos preached two years before "the earthquake" (1:1). This must have been an earthquake of some magnitude, as it is alluded to in Isa 5:25, mentioned as occurring during Uzziah's reign in Zech 14:5, and cited later by Josephus (*Ant.* 9:222–27), who connects it with Uzziah's impiety and onset of the king's scale disease (biblical "leprosy"—see 2 Kgs 15:5 and 2 Chr 26:16–20). The date of this earthquake has been put circa 760 BC, there being archaeological evidence supporting it at Hazor Stratum VI,[6] at Gath, and elsewhere.[7] This natural disaster would have given Amos's prophecy credibility, particularly in view of what he said in 8:8 and 9:1.

The compiler of Amos's book gives us other information about the prophet in chapter 7. There we are told he turned up at the Bethel sanctuary and reported a vision in which he acted as mediator of the covenant, pleading as Moses had that Yahweh would forgive Israel (cf. Exod 32:11–14; Num 11:2; etc.). His first two mediations were successful, but not the third. Yahweh said now that Israel's worship sites would be destroyed and he would rise against the house of Jeroboam with the sword (7:1–9). Amaziah, the priest at Bethel, was duly alarmed and sent word to the king that Amos had conspired against him. He then turned to Amos and told him to go home and preach there, but never again come to Bethel, for it was the king's sanctuary (7:10–13).

Amos responds to the rebuke by saying that he is not a prophet or the son of a prophet, but a simple herdsman and dresser of sycamore trees. Nevertheless, Yahweh took him from the flock and told him to go prophesy to his people

---

6. Wolff, *Joel and Amos*, 124; King, *Amos, Hosea, and Micah*, 21, 38.

7. Chadwick and Maeir, "Judahite Gath," 48–50, who estimate that this earthquake would have measured 8 on the Richter scale.

Israel. His parting word is a blistering prophecy directed to the Bethel priest: His wife would become a harlot, his sons and daughters would die by the sword, and the land would be parceled out to others. Finally, the priest like the nation would go into exile, suffering there the indignity of dying in an unclean land (7:14–17).

Hosea

Hosea's father is mentioned in the superscription to his book, but that is all we are given of a personal nature: Hosea was the son of Beeri (1:1). We know not what city or town he came from, nor any place where he prophesied. The superscription does say that he preached in the days of Uzziah, Jotham, Ahaz, and Hezekiah, kings of Judah, repeating kings named in the superscription to Isaiah (Isa 1:1), but adding Jeroboam, son of Joash, king of Israel. This could give a beginning to his ministry circa 750 BC, the ending being uncertain. Jeroboam died in 746, and Israel's last kings were not worth mentioning. Samaria fell to the Assyrians in 722. If Hosea survived the fall of the north, he could still have been alive during Hezekiah's reign, which began in 715. In his book are numerous references to Judah, one hope passage looking forward to a unified Israel under a Davidic king (3:5). But of Hosea's final days we know nothing. Hosea is taken to be Northern Israel's only homegrown prophet, although this is assumed only from the content of his judgment oracles, all of which are against Northern Israel. Hosea probably did his preaching in Samaria, but again this is only a surmise. No oracles against foreign nations are in his book.

The compiler of the book of Hosea does provide some information about the prophet in chapters 1–3, where we learn that he was commanded by Yahweh to act out his prophecy twice in symbolic action. These chapters have been much discussed, as interpretation is difficult, but some clarity can be achieved once we see how the material is structured. It is arranged in a way known to be common among ancient Hebrew scribes, where the beginning and end are balanced, and climactic material comes in the center. Hosea at beginning and end is told by Yahweh to engage in symbolic action—i.e., to take a promiscuous woman as a wife (1:2–9; 3:1–5). These passages are not allegory, as some allege; they are real experiences in the life of the prophet. At the center is a core message in which Yahweh speaks directly to Israel about its promiscuous behavior of going after other gods and forsaking Yahweh (2:2–25). A correlation between this message and the prophet's symbolic action does exist, but it is not exact, and the two must not be harmonized. The overall structure is filled out by hope prophecies for Israel, Judah, and all creation in 1:10—2:1 and 2:16–23.

Things begin by Yahweh commanding Hosea to marry a woman of harlotry and have children of harlotry, which he does (1:2–9). The woman is already a harlot, not one with a potential for harlotry, since the command is that she also bear children of harlotry. This will convey to Israel the message that it has committed great harlotry by forsaking Yahweh. What happened to this marriage we are not told. Gomer could have left Hosea; Hosea could have divorced her; we simply do not know. The writer is not interested in telling us. Also, it is by no means clear that Gomer is the woman Hosea remarries in 3:1–2. Hosea could have married another woman.

What follows in 1:10—2:1 is hope for a later time, but we are finished with symbolic action. This is simply a message reversing the symbolic action, promising hope to a united Israel and Judah in the future. At the center is a core message consisting most likely of two separate oracles in which Yahweh speaks directly to Israel about its waywardness (2:2–13, 14–15). The RSV and NRSV rightly format this as poetry, making it read like the rest of Hosea's preaching in the book. Following is a couple more hope messages, one announcing a future covenant Yahweh will make between Israel and all creation, which will allow Israel to live in safety (2:16–20, 21–23). Its conclusion even more completely reverses Hosea's symbolic actions than 1:10—2:1.

The introduction concludes with Yahweh commanding Hosea to again marry an immoral woman, this time one said to be an adulteress, but now to keep her at home so she does not go out and play the whore (3:1–5). Here the prophet speaks in the first person. The woman is often taken to be Gomer, but since Hosea pays either a slave price (see Exod 21:32) or a bridal price of fifteen shekels of silver to get her, she could be another woman entirely. This is to symbolize Israel's survival after its loss of nationhood, and its return to Yahweh under a Davidic king. The structure of chapters 1–3 is then a nice chiasmus:

  a Yahweh's command that Hosea marry a woman of harlotry (1:2–9)

     b Message of future hope to a united Israel and Judah (1:10—2:1)

        c Yahweh's direct speech to wayward Israel (2:2–15)

     b' Messages of future hope including a covenant with creation (2:16–23)

  a' Yahweh's command that Hosea marry an adulterous woman (3:1–5)

Hosea expresses the covenant in marital and familial terms: Yahweh and Israel are husband and wife, father and son. As for the marriage, it has gone bad because Israel has broken the Sinai covenant. Hosea's first recorded preaching in 2:2–15 builds on his symbolic action. In Hosea we perceive a softer tone than in the hard-hitting Amos or the blunt Micah, which may go some way in explaining why his preaching has bona fide hope following judgment.

The text of Hosea is difficult, and in many cases we do not know precisely what the prophet is saying. However, some of the difficulties can be overcome once we realize that the poetry shifts often from the metaphorical to the literal, and it changes both speaker and audience, accounting for many alternations of singular and plural pronouns.

Micah

About Micah we also know very little. The superscription to his book tells us only that he came from Moresheth. Moresheth was a small town near Gath (called Moresheth-Gath in 1:14), located in the Shephelah, the foothills between the Judahite highlands and the coastal plain. It lay six miles northeast of the larger and more important city of Lachish. The ancient site has been identified since the 1930s with modern Tell el-Judeideh, excavated briefly by F. J. Bliss and R. A. Macalister in 1899–1900.[8] The site is a natural hill circa 398 meters above sea level.

Because nothing is said about his family, some think Micah came from a peasant background, but we do not know if this was the case. He is nevertheless widely regarded as a simple man from the country who recognized and condemned inhuman behavior of the ruling classes in his day (3:1–4). In him the oppressed poor found an advocate against the overbearing rich (2:1–2, 8–9; 3:3, 9–10). Some think he was influenced by Amos. Micah attacked in blunt

8. Luker, "Moresheth," 904.

language not only social injustices but also the deplorable religious conditions of his time. Prophets and priests received strong condemnation (3:5, 11); like Amos, he stood apart from other recognized prophets of his day (3:5). Micah also railed against corrupt judges (7:3) and dishonest merchants in the marketplace (6:11).

The superscription says that Micah preached concerning Jerusalem and Samaria during the reigns of Jotham, Ahaz, and Hezekiah, kings of Judah. He would then have been a contemporary of Isaiah. Only a small amount of Micah's prophecy concerns Northern Israel; the bulk of his preaching is against Judah. But saying that Yahweh "will make Samaria a heap in the open country" (1:6) would put his early ministry before the fall of Samaria in 722 BC and make him a younger contemporary of Amos and Hosea. Micah makes no specific mention of the Assyrian invasion of the north (but see 5:5–6 in a prophecy about the future), and nothing specific is said about Sennacherib's invasion of Judah in 701.

We learn nothing more about this prophet from the book bearing his name, but something does appear about Micah in the book of Jeremiah (Jer 26:17–19). When Jeremiah is on trial for preaching his scorching "temple oracles" of 609 BC, elders present at the trial rise up in Jeremiah's defense, pointing out that Micah had preached judgment against Jerusalem in the days of Hezekiah (Mic 3:12), and that king (with all Judah) did not put him to death. Micah's preaching had good effect. Hezekiah feared Yahweh and "softened Yahweh's face" (cf. 2 Kgs 19:14–19; Isa 37:14–20), with the result that evil planned for Jerusalem was rescinded. Micah's prophecy therefore went unfulfilled. Hezekiah's reform could also have been in response to Micah's preaching.

Micah also contains hopeful preaching, the most important of which appears in the center of his book (4:1—5:15). Other restoration preaching is interspersed between indictment and judgment (2:12–13). Preaching on the wait for salvation, divine forgiveness, and Israel's return to faithfulness in 7:8–20 may or may not be from Micah. The hope prophecy in 4:1–3 appears also in Isa 2:2–4.

REFLECTION

1. Do you agree with Heschel that the prophets take us to the slums?

2. How would you respond to the hard-hitting prophecies of Amos? Should preachers speak this way from church pulpits, or is it better suited for out in the streets?

3. How do you feel about Hosea's symbolic action of marrying a promiscuous woman, and might this help to explain the softer tone of his preaching?

4. Does Micah's promise of a future king the likes of David have only one fulfillment in Jesus, or might it have had earlier fulfillment in his time?

AMOS

3

"YAHWEH ROARS FROM ZION" (AMOS 1:2—3:8) [1]

1 ²And he said:
  Yahweh from Zion roars
    and from Jerusalem he utters his voice
  And the pastures of the shepherds mourn
    and the top of Carmel withers.

³Thus said Yahweh:
  For three transgressions of Damascus
    and for four, I will not revoke it
  For with threshing sleds of iron
    they threshed Gilead
⁴So I will send a fire on the house of Hazael
    and it shall devour the strongholds of Ben-hadad
⁵And I will break the gate bars of Damascus
    and cut off the inhabitant from the Valley of Aven

1. Unless otherwise noted, all biblical translations are mine.

And the one who holds the scepter from Beth-eden
   and the people of Aram shall be exiled to Kir
         said Yahweh.

6Thus said Yahweh:
  For three transgressions of Gaza
    and for four, I will not revoke it
  For they took into exile an entire people
    to deliver up to Edom
7So I will send a fire against the wall of Gaza
    and it shall devour her strongholds
8And I will cut off the inhabitant from Ashdod
    and the one who holds the scepter from Ashkelon
And I will turn my hand against Ekron
    and the remnant of the Philistines shall perish
        said Lord Yahweh

9Thus said Yahweh:
  For three transgressions of Tyre
    and for four, I will not revoke it
  Because they delivered up an entire people to Edom
    and did not remember the covenant of brotherhood
10So I will send a fire against the wall of Tyre
    and it shall devour her strongholds.

11Thus said Yahweh
  For three transgressions of Edom
    and for four, I will not revoke it
  For he pursued his brother with the sword
    and abandoned his compassion
  Yes, his anger tore perpetually
    and his rage he kept forever
12So I will send a fire against Teman
    and it shall devour the strongholds of Bozrah.

13 *Thus said Yahweh*
   For three transgressions of the Ammonites
      and for four, I will not revoke it
   For they ripped open pregnant women in Gilead
      in order to enlarge their border
14 *So I will kindle a fire against the wall of Rabbah*
      and it shall devour her strongholds
   With shouting on the day of battle
      with a storm on the day of the whirlwind
15 *And their king shall go into exile*
      he and his princes together
                        said Yahweh.

2 1 *Thus said Yahweh:*
   For three transgressions of Moab
      and for four, I will not revoke it
   For he burned the bones
      of the king of Edom to lime
2 *So I will send a fire against Moab*
      and it shall devour the strongholds of Kerioth
   And Moab shall die in uproar
      in shouting with the sound of the trumpet
3 *And I will cut off the ruler from its midst*
      and all her officials I will kill with him
                        said Yahweh.

4 *Thus said Yahweh:*
   For three transgressions of Judah
      and for four, I will not revoke it
   For they have rejected the law of Yahweh
      and its statutes they have not kept
   And their lies have led them astray
      after which their ancestors walked

5So I will send a fire against Judah
   and it shall devour the strongholds of Jerusalem

6Thus said Yahweh:
 For three transgressions of Israel
   and for four, I will not revoke it
 For they sell the righteous for silver
   and the needy for a pair of sandals
7They who tamp upon loose soil of the earth with the
head of the poor
   and push aside the way of the afflicted
 And a man and his father go into the maiden
   so that my holy name is profaned
8And upon garments taken in pledge they lay themselves
down
   beside every altar
 And they drink the wine of those who have been fined
   in the house of their God
9Yet I, I destroyed the Amorite before them
   whose height was like the height of cedars
    and who was as strong as the oaks
 And I destroyed his fruit from above
   and his roots from beneath
10Also I, I brought you up out of the land of Egypt
   and I led you in the wilderness forty years
    to possess the land of the Amorite
11And I raised up some of your sons to be prophets
   and some of your young men to be Nazirites
    Is not it indeed so, O people of Israel?
        oracle of Yahweh.
12But you made the Nazirites drink wine
   and the prophets you commanded
    saying, "You shall not prophesy"

13*Behold, I will press you down in your place*
 just as the cart presses down
  when it is full of sheaves
14*And flight shall perish from the swift*
 and the strong shall not retain his strength
  and the mighty shall not escape with his life
15*And he who handles the bow shall not stand*
 and he who is swift of foot shall not escape
  and he who rides the horse shall not escape with his
  life
16*And he who is stout of heart among the mighty*
 shall flee away naked in that day
            oracle of Yahweh.

3 1*Hear this word that Yahweh has spoken against you, O*
people of Israel, against the whole family that I brought up
out of the land of Egypt:
 2*Only you have I known*
  of all the families of the earth
  Therefore I will visit upon you
   all your iniquities.

 3*Do two walk together*
  unless they have made an appointment?
 4*Does a lion roar in the forest*
  when it has no prey?
  Does a young lion cry out from his den
   if it has caught nothing?
 5*Does a bird fall into a snare on the earth*
  when there is no trap for it?
  Does a snare spring up from the ground
   when it has taken nothing?

⁶*Is a trumpet blown in the city*
  and people are not afraid?
 Does evil happen to a city
  when Yahweh has not done it?
⁷*Surely Lord Yahweh does nothing without revealing his*
secret to his servants the prophets.

⁸*The Lion has roared*
  who will not fear?
 Lord Yahweh has spoken
  who will not prophesy?

HERE AT THE BEGINNING of the book of Amos is a rhetorical structure in 1:2—3:8 that has been broken up and obscured by a "Hear this word . . ." introduction in 3:1, brought in most likely by a scribe to correspond with "Hear this word . . ." introductions in 4:1 and 5:1. The structure is also obscured by the later divisions into chapters 2 and 3. In this discourse the prophet begins by announcing Yahweh's roar from Zion (1:2), and concludes by saying that because of this roar he has no choice but to prophesy (3:8). The tie-in between beginning and end makes an inclusio. But a closer look at the entire unit reveals a nice chiasmus:

a   Amos hears Yahweh *roar* from Zion   1:2

   b   Yahweh speaks *seven* oracles
       against the nations   1:3—2:5

       Yahweh speaks an oracle
       against Israel   (+1)   2:6–16

     c   Yahweh states the terms
         of the Sinai covenant   3:2

b'	Amos gives *seven* set-up rhetorical questions		3:3–6
	Amos authenticates Yahweh's prophets	(+1)	3:7
a'	Amos validates his call from the *roaring* Lion		3:8

The discourse has a 7 + 1 pattern in b and b', which is conventional in Canaanite and Israelite literature. The numbers 3 and 3 + 1, 7 and 7 + 1, signify completeness. We see it again in the stereotypical "for three transgressions . . . and for four" beginning each oracle against the nation (3 and 3 + 1 = 7). For 7 and 8 (= 7 + 1) in parallelism, see also Mic 5:5. Enumerations in a 7 or 7 + 1 pattern occur with unusual frequency in Amos:

1. the 7 + 1 list of nations to be judged in 1:3—2:16

2. the 7 transgressions of Israel in 2:6–8

3. the 7 acts of punishment for Israel in 2:14–16

4. the 7 + 1 series of rhetorical questions in 3:3–8

5. the 7 verbs ironically calling for sanctuary worship in 4:4–5

6. the 7 prior calamities sent by Yahweh in 4:6–12

7. the 7 verbs in the hymnic fragment of 5:8–9

8. the 7 things Yahweh hates in 5:21–24

9. the 7 verbs calling for woe in 6:4–6

10. the 7 damning quotes from the merchants in 8:5–8

There is also a rhetorical structure in the eight oracles against the nations (1:3—2:16), which taken in sequence form a crosswise pattern following the points of the compass:

(3) Tyre   (1) Damascus

(8) Israel   (5) Ammon

X

(7) Judah   (6) Moab

(2) Gaza   (4) Edom

If Amos can be imagined standing somewhere between Samaria and Jerusalem—perhaps at Bethel, the one location where he is known to have preached (7:10–13)—his recitation of oracles while facing in the direction of each nation would be drama of a high order. He may have even smashed pottery as each nation was addressed, which was done in public denunciations in Egypt. The masterful survey ends right where the prophet intends: with Israel. If the audience has given hearty assent to judgment on seven other nations, including Judah, it cannot stop the momentum and refrain from judging Israel, which it will be reluctant to do. The audience, which is Northern Israelite, has been trapped, and the prophet's objective has been achieved. This surprise element is a signature of Amos. We see it again in Yahweh's word to Israel in 3:2.

Oracles against the nations begin with a stereotyped indictment:

> For three transgressions of _____
>
> and for four, I will not revoke it.

The numerical progression "for three . . . and for four" indicates an indefinite number (Prov 30:15, 18, 21, 29; Eccl

11:2; Mic 5:5). All the oracles except the one against Israel contain variations of a stereotyped judgment:

> So I will send / kindle a fire against
> (the wall / the house of) _____
>
> and it shall devour the strongholds of _____/
> her strongholds.

The lack of a stereotyped judgment against Israel can be explained as a deliberate deviation from an established pattern (cf. Jer 50:35–38: swords—drought), replaced here by a different type of judgment oracle (2:12–16). This judgment against Israel may in fact combine two originally separate oracles, for there are two "oracle of Yahweh" formulas concluding vv. 11 and 16.

Foreign nations are judged for gross inhumanity toward one another; Judah and Israel are judged for covenant violation, assumed also climactically at the center of the discourse (3:2). We see here at the outset Amos's universalistic outlook: Israel's God is God of the entire world. This universalism is shown again in 9:7, where the prophet says that while Yahweh brought up Israel from the land of Egypt, did he not also bring up the Philistines from Caphtor and the Syrians from Kir? Yahweh has been engaged in a wide-ranging moving business!

YAHWEH ROARS FROM ZION (AMOS 1:2)

Amos begins his masterful discourse by announcing Yahweh's roar from Zion. It is the roar of a lion (3:4, 8; Isa 5:29), "lion" being the common metaphor for an enemy throughout the ANE, used frequently by the prophets (Hos 5:14; Isa 5:26–30; Jer 2:15; 4:7; 5:6; Ezek 32:2). Zion is Jerusalem, and Amos betrays his identity as a Judahite for whom the temple is the place where Yahweh chooses to make his name reside (Deut 12:5, 11; 14:23–24; 16:2; etc.). The prophet Joel repeats the first part of the verse, only with him the roar precedes a word of hope (Joel 3:16). When Yahweh roars, the pastures of the shepherds mourn and the top of Carmel withers. "Mourning pastures" are pastures turned brown for lack of water (cf. Jer 12:4). Carmel is one of Israel's prominent mountains overlooking the Mediterranean at present-day Haifa, noted for its fertility, orchards, and forests.

YAHWEH ROARS TO THE NATIONS (AMOS 1:3—2:16)

Yahweh's Word to Syria (Amos 1:3–5)

Yahweh intends judgment for Syria, which in the Bible is called Aram, and he will not revoke it. The capital of Syria is Damascus (Isa 7:8). In the mid-eighth century, until the rise of Assyria, Syria was Northern Israel's major antagonist (Isa 7–8). Isaiah also prophesied against Damascus (Isa 8:4; 17:1–6). Syria was guilty of numberless transgressions, but the one cited here was threshing the people of Gilead with threshing sleds, which had sharp pieces of iron underneath. In Egypt and Israel these were pulled by animals to separate grain from chaff (2 Sam 24:22). War is cruel, but this was brutal torture. Gilead was a territory in Transjordan between the Yarmuk River in the north and Heshbon in the south. This atrocity could have taken place in Hazael's conquest of Gilead recorded in 2 Kgs 10:32–33.

For this cruelty and for others, Yahweh will send a fire on the house of Hazael, destroying the strongholds of Ben-hadad (cf. Jer 49:27). Hazael (r. 842–806 BC) and his son Ben-hadad II (r. 806–) were kings of Syria reigning in Damascus (2 Kgs 8:7–15; 13:24). Fire is a stock image of judgment (2 Kgs 1:10, 12, 14). Strongholds were towers at corners of city walls where people would seek refuge when the wall fell, and setting fire to them was a way of forcing them out. City gates had bars to keep them securely closed, but the bars of Damascus will be broken by the enemy (Nah 3:13; Jer 51:30; Lam 2:9). The "inhabitant" (singular) "of Aven" could denote the one sitting on the throne. The Valley of Aven (= Valley of Wickedness) is the Beqaa Valley between the Lebanon and anti-Lebanon mountains (Baalbeck), which had become a place of idolatry. Beth-eden was an Aramaic city-state between the Euphrates and the Balikh Rivers, about two hundred miles northeast of Damascus (modern Tel Barsip). It could also be the Bit Adini of Assyrian inscriptions, a Syrian city on the Euphrates. A "people of Eden" were conquered by the Assyrians according to 2 Kgs 19:12 (Isa 37:12). The people of Syria will be exiled to Kir, which is where they came from (9:7). Yahweh will reverse their migration! Kir is a Mesopotamian locality, perhaps near Elam (Isa 22:6), but is unknown. The Assyrian king Tiglath-pileser III exiled the Syrians to Kir in circa 732 BC (2 Kgs 16:9).

The idea of Yahweh's moral government of the world is reflected in Deut 9:4–5, where Israel is told that Yahweh will drive out Canaan's former inhabitants because of their wickedness. Before this was the Great Flood (Gen 6:5–7) and Yahweh's destruction of Sodom and Gomorrah (Gen 18:20—19:29). The entire Primeval History (Gen 1–11), in fact, has Yahweh bringing judgment on non-Israelite people because of disobedience (Adam and Eve), jealousy and murder (Cain), wicked living (the Great Flood), and hubris (Babel).

Yahweh's Word to the Philistines (Amos 1:6–8)

Next to be dealt with by Yahweh are the Philistines. Gaza is one of four remaining cities of Philistia along with Ashdod, Ashkelon, and Ekron of the earlier pentapolis (Josh 13:2–3; Zeph 2:4; Jer 25:20). The fifth was Gath, made famous by the mighty Goliath (1 Sam 17:4, 23). It was destroyed by Hazael in the ninth century (2 Kgs 12:17). Archaeological finds, however, point to it being a Judahite city in the mid-eighth century. The Chronicler reports that Uzziah broke down its walls (2 Chr 26:6), presumably early in his reign, and if he rebuilt the city, which is not known for sure, it would have become Judahite. Around 760 BC an earthquake shook the entire region (Amos 1:1), and archaeology has turned up evidence of it at Gath. Amos and Micah refer to the city, but Amos calls it Philistine, probably because it was then a ruin (Amos 6:2; Mic 1:10). Isaiah also gives an oracle against the Philistines (Isa 14:29–31).

The Philistines come in for censure because they delivered up an entire people to Edom. The Philistines were known to be mercenaries (cf. Joel 3:4–6), but this is slave trading on a large scale. Slaves were evidently procured for the Edomites to sell to someone else. The Tyrians did the same thing (Amos 1:9). Exiles sold to Edom were probably put to work in the copper mines of Edom. Gaza is a fortified city, so Yahweh will send a fire against its walls. Inhabitants of Ashdod and the ruler of Ashkelon will be cut off. Yahweh will also turn his hand against Ekron, making the Philistine demise complete. "Turning the hand against" is an expression of judgment (Isa 1:25). There will be no remnant for the Philistines (cf. Ezek 25:15–17).

Yahweh's Word to the Phoenicians (Amos 1:9–10)

Tyre was the most important commercial city of Phoenicia. The other important city was Sidon (Isa 23:2, 4, 12). The transgression of this coastal nation north of Israel is the same as that of Gaza: slave trading on a large scale. Phoenicians were known to be involved in slave trade (Ezek 27:13; Joel 3:6–7). Isaiah also gave an oracle against Tyre (Isa 23).

Tyre is censured also for not remembering a covenant of brotherhood. If Israel was the treaty partner, this could refer to the pact between Solomon and Hiram of Tyre (1 Kgs 5:12), but it could also be a treaty between Tyre and some non-Israelite nation. Treaty partners are called "brothers" (1 Kgs 9:13). Tyre too will see a fire on her walls that will destroy her strongholds.

Yahweh's Word to Edom (Amos 1:11–12)

Edom (Esau) was a brother to Israel, a tribe now residing in the highlands of Seir (Gen 26:8). Edom means "red" in Hebrew, probably referring to red sandstone in the area (Petra). Edom lies south of Moab, extending from the River Zered down to the eastern finger of the Red Sea (the present-day Gulf of Aqaba). Through the middle of the country runs the ancient King's Highway.

In spite of the reconciliation between the two brothers (Gen 33), early tension persisted. Amos says that Edom pursued his brother with the sword (Amos 1:11; cf. Gen 27:40). The incident referred to could have been in the mid-ninth century when Edom attained independence during the reign of Jehoram (2 Kgs 8:16–20). More recently Uzziah (Azariah) took Elath, an Edomite city (2 Kgs 14:22), probably indicating more strife between the two nations. Edom later rejoiced over the fall of Jerusalem, and Israel did not forget it (Ps 137:7; Obad 9-14; Ezek 35:15). But ongoing tension existed long before (Exod 17:8-16; Judg 10:12). Reference could be to some excessive act of cruelty in war, also to Amalek, a grandson of Esau (Gen 36:12), who took advantage of Israel on the journey out of Egypt by attacking the sick, wounded, and weary who lagged behind, and were unable to keep up with the others. Amos says Edom's anger raged forever. We know that Israel's rage against Amalek was not to be forgotten (Deut 25:17-19; 1 Sam 15:2; cf. Num 14:43-45; 24:20). In Deuteronomy we see a kinder attitude toward the Edomites (Deut 23:7).

Judgment on Edom will be a fire sent against Teman, which will destroy the strongholds of Bozrah. Teman was a district in northeast Edom, the dwelling of a clan by the same name descended from Esau (Gen 36:11, 15; Ezek 25:13). Teman had a reputation for wisdom (Jer 49:7). Job's friend Eliphaz was a Temanite (Job 2:11; 4:1). Bozrah was an Edomite fortress twenty-three miles south-southeast of the Dead Sea and thirty-five miles north of Petra (modern Buseirah, Jordan). It was Edom's major city, possibly its capital. Isaiah also prophesied against Edom (Isa 34:5-7).

Yahweh's Word to the Ammonites (Amos 1:13–15)

The Ammonites were a Transjordanian tribal people living north of Moab. Their capital city was Rabbah (present-day Amman, Jordan), which was up over the mountains nearly twenty-five miles east of the Jordan River. The Ammonites were known for cruel behavior in war (1 Sam 11), cited here for ripping open pregnant women in Gilead. Elisha predicted that Hazael and the Syrians would do this (2 Kgs 8:12), and they did (Amos 1:3). Menahem, one of the last violent kings of Israel, also ripped open pregnant women in war (2 Kgs 15:16). Hosea predicted the same cruelty for

Samaria when its time came (Hos 13:16). The Ammonites at some point expanded their territory into Gilead, perhaps filling a vacuum after Tiglath-Pileser III overran Transjordan in 734 BC and deported remaining Israelites to Assyria. This has Amos preaching after his ministry began between 760 and 750.

Yahweh's judgment of the Ammonites is that a fire will be kindled against the wall of Rabbah, its capital (Deut 3:11; Josh 13:25). There will be shouting and a great tempest the day Ammon is defeated. Attacking armies gave an anticipatory shout to inspire the ranks and intimidate the enemy (Josh 6:10, 16; 1 Sam 17:52). Whirlwind is another metaphor of divine judgment (Jer 23:19; 25:32). Ammon's king and his princes will go into exile. Deuteronomy has no love for the Ammonites, excluding them permanently from Yahweh's assembly for not giving Israelites food and water on their way out of Egypt (Deut 23:3–6).

Yahweh's Word to Moab (Amos 2:1–3)

Moab occupied the high plateau region east of the Dead Sea, its northern boundary being the spectacular canyon at the base of which lay the River Arnon (modern Wadi al-Mūjib), its southern boundary the no less spectacular canyon containing the River Zered (modern Wadi el-ḥasā). Through the center of Moab ran the King's Highway. Moab is judged because it burned the bones of the king of Edom to lime (cf. Isa 33:12). This reduced the body to ashes possibly to make plaster (so the Targum). Lime was used for plastering over stone, creating a surface on which one could write legibly (cf. Deut 27:2, 4). The custom was Egyptian. Burning the remains of anyone was done only rarely in the ANE, where burial was the norm. It was a monstrous act of desecration to burn the body of the deceased (Gen 38:24;

Judg 15:6), something quite different from the practice in the Far East, and what is being done increasingly today in America.

Fire will also descend upon Moab and devour the strongholds of Kerioth, presumably its capital. Kerioth is believed to have been a fortified city, thirteen miles south of modern-day Madeba, although the site is unknown. Mention is made of it in Jer 48:24, also on the Moabite Stone (line 13) where its mention appears to be as a cult center of Chemosh. Moab too will die amid uproar, shouting, and the sound of the trumpet—all sounds of war (Hos 10:14). The ruler, which could also be translated "judge," makes a wordplay in Hebrew with "trumpet" in the prior verse. Isaiah also prophesies against Moab (Isa 15–16; 25:10b–12). Deuteronomy has no love for Moab because Balak, the Moabite king, hired Balaam the seer to curse Israel (Deut 23:3–6).

Yahweh's Word to Judah (Amos 2:4–5)

With this prophecy we are coming closer to home. Actually we are at home, for Amos resides in Judah. Judah is censured not because of any inhumane or moral outrage, but because it has rejected the law (*torah*) of Yahweh and not kept its statutes. This is every bit as serious, probably more so in the eyes of the prophet. Deuteronomy has Moses telling the covenant people that they must be sure to "keep the commandments, the statutes, and the ordinances" once they become settled in the land (Deut 4:1; 8:11; etc.). If they do not, the covenant curses will fall (Deut 28). Lies leading people astray are probably idols, which have been around in Israel a long time, since Sinai when Aaron and the Israelites made a golden calf. There are now calves at the sanctuaries of Dan and Bethel (1 Kgs 12:28–30; Hos 8:4–6; 13:2).

Jeremiah later calls Baal "the Lie" (Jer 3:23; 5:2.31). A fire will also descend upon Judah, devouring the strongholds of Jerusalem.

Yahweh's Word to Israel (Amos 2:6–16)

Now we have come to Amos's preferred subject: Israel, the Northern Kingdom. People there are selling the righteous poor for silver and the needy for a pair of shoes (8:6). They are turning the poor on their heads and tamping the earth with them, having no time for the afflicted. The tamping image is unusual. Threshing floors are not used nine or ten months of the year, only during harvest when they were smoothed and hardened by tamping. The verb translated "tamp" otherwise means "to crush, trample upon" (cf. 8:4). Pushing aside the way (= road) of the afflicted means perverting justice (Deut 16:19; 24:17; 27:19). Job talks about the wicked who "thrust the needy off the road" (Job 24:4). Wealthy creditors are oppressing the poor with loans in silver and then foreclosing at harvest for nonpayment.

Amos is here lashing out against social injustices in the north (4:1; 5:11–12; 8:4–6), just as Micah is condemning the same in the south (Mic 2:1–2; 3:1–3, 9–12). Deuteronomy says there must be no oppression of the poor and needy; they must be shown justice, benevolence, and generosity (Deut 1:16; 15:1–12, 14; 23:19–20; 24:6–7, 10–15, 17–18). The needy are people poor in material goods and often powerless to do anything about it.

Men in Israel are also guilty of moral offenses. A man and his father are having sex with the same young girl. This could refer to sacral prostitution, which Deuteronomy condemns (Deut 23:17), or the woman could be an ordinary harlot. Amos does not cite sexual indiscretion as much as

Hosea does, but here he does censure it. Doing this profanes the holy name of Yahweh.

Another injustice was sleeping on garments of the poor taken in pledge. Pledges were distraints for unpaid debts, permitted so debtors would quicken repayments of money, grain, seed for grain, and other borrowed items. They could consist of almost any of the debtor's property, with hand-mills and upper millstones being exceptions. These were disallowed since taking them would be tantamount to taking a person's life. A working mill was necessary for grinding flour and making daily bread (Deut 24:6). Garments were commonly taken as pledges (Prov 20:16; 27:13), but laws protected widows and the poor. The garment of a poor person had to be returned before sundown so he or she could sleep in it (Exod 22:26–27; Deut 24:12–13). Ezekiel considered the restoring of a pledge a life-and-death issue for the creditor (Ezek 18:7, 12; 33:15). Not to restore was robbery. As for a widow's garment, it could not under any circumstances be taken as a pledge (Deut 24:17). What was going on here was that creditors were not returning garments of the poor taken in pledge, and were reclining in them beside altars to give their unjust act a measure of legitimacy. Those callously seizing garments from the poor came in for strong censure (Job 22:6).

The wicked were also drinking wine of those who had been fined in the sanctuary (2:8), another attempt to legitimize some unjust act. These were probably fixed fines (cf. Deut 22:19), taken unjustly by priests for their own benefit. Priests given to greed were known ever since the days of Eli and his sons at the Shiloh sanctuary (1 Sam 2:12–17). "Their God" in Amos 2:8 creates distance between the priests and Yahweh (cf. "your calf" in Hos 8:5).

Yahweh then proceeds to give Israel a history lesson, the purpose of which is to contrast Israel's present crimes with his own goodness to the nation in years past (2:9–12). With emphasis Yahweh says that it was he who destroyed the Amorites to give Israel its land. The emphatic "I" should not go unnoticed. The Amorites were Canaan's prior inhabitants (Gen 15:16, 21; Deut 1:44; 7:1). Their height was like the height of cedars (Amos 2:9)—a bit of hyperbole, similar to what the spies reported after scoping out the land (Deut 1:28). And yes, this giant race was as strong as oaks, which the Israelites discovered to their sorrow in their first attempt to enter the land (Deut 1:44). Yet in the end Yahweh destroyed this formidable foe completely (Josh 24:8). The merism strives after totality.

Yahweh then calls to mind his earlier and defining act of divine grace, namely the bringing up of Israel from the land of Egypt (another emphatic "I"), after which Yahweh says he led Israel forty years in the wilderness in order to possess the land of the Amorites (Deut 32:10–12). The poetry in Amos 2:9–10 has a tie-in between beginning and end with a repetition of the term "Amorite."

Yahweh then reminds Israel that he raised up some of its sons to be prophets, also some to be Nazirites. Was it not so (Amos 2:11)? Nazirites were an ascetic group protesting the settled life, vowing not to cut their hair, drink wine, or have contact with the dead during their period of separation (Num 6). Samson and Samuel were both Nazirites (Judg 13; 16:17; 1 Sam 1:11).

The second oracle follows through on Yahweh's raising up of prophets and Nazirites, turning now to judgment. Here we see a nice chiasmus in the poetry of vv. 11–12: "prophets : Nazirites : Nazirites : prophets." How did people respond to these individuals raised up by Yahweh? Well, they made the Nazirites drink wine, which violated their vow, and told the prophets not to prophesy. Amos himself was told not to prophesy at Bethel (Amos 7:12–13, 16), and the same rebuke was heard by Micah (Mic 2:6). Jeremiah in his time was told not to prophesy in the way he was doing (Jer 11:21; 26:9, 11). But Deuteronomy said Yahweh would continue raising up prophets (Deut 18:15–22).

Well, there is going to be punishment for all this, and it will be no less severe than the fire sent to devour the strongholds of Samaria. Doom awaits Israel. People will be pressed down in their place as a cart presses down when full of sheaves (Amos 2:13). Sheaves are newly cut grain (cf. Jer 9:22). The cart is overloaded and may actually have collapsed. Whatever the precise meaning of this image, people will be prevented from moving, and almost no one will escape (cf. Job 11:20): the swift of foot will be unable to flee (Amos 2:14; cf. Jer 46:6); the strong will become weak; the mighty will not escape with his life; archers will be casualties; horsemen in flight will not save their lives. The stoutest among the mighty will flee away naked in that day, which is a coming day of Yahweh (3:14; 5:18–20). Amos speaks about an inability to escape Yahweh's wrath in 9:1–4. The end has come for Israel (7:8; 8:2). The present verses have nice balance, repetition, and a chiasmus in the words "flight : mighty : mighty : flee." Judgment also seems to befit the crime, with the pressing down of the wicked in v. 13 paralleling the tamping of the poor by the same in v. 7.

BUT ISRAEL IS SPECIAL (AMOS 3:2)

Here at the center of this well-constructed prophecy comes the weightiest pronouncement of all (3:2). The expanded messenger formula in 3:1, with its reminder of Yahweh's deliverance of Israel in the exodus from Egypt, is a later addition (cf. 5:1). Amos otherwise downplays the exodus (cf. 9:7). But here Yahweh says Israel is special: "Only you have I known of all the families of the earth." "Families" means nations (Jer 1:15; 15:3; 10:25; 25:9). Israel is Yahweh's first-born son (Exod 4:22–23), his chosen one (Deut 4:20; 7:6–8; 9:26, 29; 10:15; 32:8–9). Yahweh has known only Israel, and Israel has known only Yahweh (Hos 13:4).

Then comes the surprise. Because Israel is special, Yahweh will punish her. Should not Yahweh rather go easy on a people who are special? No. Deuteronomy teaches that Israel will be punished for disobeying the commandments (Deut 7:4, 10; 11:28; 28:15–68), and Amos speaks elsewhere about Yahweh punishing Israel (3:14). Here the prophet is disrupting audience expectation.

QUESTIONS TO BE ANSWERED (AMOS 3:3–7)

Amos now poses in a mechanical sort of way seven rhetorical questions for his audience to answer. He does it again in 6:12. The questions here are a setup for a double question with which the prophecy concludes (3:8). These questions are the following:

> Do two walk together unless they have made an appointment? Of course not!

> Does a lion roar in the forest when it has no prey? Of course not! (Ps 104:21).

> Does a young lion cry out from his den if it has caught nothing? Of course not!

> Does a bird fall into a snare when there is no trap for it? Of course not! Birds are caught with the aid of blinds, snares, and clapnets (Ps 124:7; Prov 7:23; Jer 5:26–27).

> Does a snare spring up when it has taken nothing? Of course not!

> Is a trumpet blown in the city and people not afraid? Of course not! The trumpet is a ram's horn with a frightful

sound, warning of an approaching enemy (Jer 4:5, 19; 6:1; Joel 2:1).

Does evil happen to a city when Yahweh has not done it? Of course not! Asked here is a question about which the entire prophecy is concerned.

This portion of prophecy concludes with a positive declaration that Yahweh does nothing without revealing his secret to his servants the prophets. On Yahweh revealing secrets to prophets in divine council, see Jer 23:18, 21–22. All of God's great works begin in secret (Jer 33:3; Ps 139:13–16).

AMOS'S CALL TO PROPHESY (AMOS 3:8)

We return now to the roar of Yahweh stated at the beginning (1:2), with Amos citing it to validate his call to prophesy. "Lion" is used here as a pure metaphor for Yahweh, an unusual coinage. Amos is saying that if the Lion has roared, if Lord Yahweh has spoken, who will not prophesy? He knows the answer. Will those hearing his words know it? Amos as a sheep breeder from Tekoa certainly knows the roar of a lion (1:1; 7:14–15).

REFLECTION

1. Do you like hard-hitting preaching about a God who is roaring from his dwelling place? Maybe out in the streets, but in a service of worship?

2. The OT teaches that anger must not be kept forever, and that even Yahweh does not keep his anger forever. What then about Moses's command in Deut 25:19 that Israel never forget the treachery of Amalek? And what

about the claim of modern Jews that we must never forget the Holocaust?

3. How do you treat your own children, who are special? Do you punish them for wrongdoing? What about the teaching in Prov 23:13–14?

4. Do you believe that all of God's great works begin in secret? If so, give some examples.

4

"PREPARE TO MEET YOUR GOD" (AMOS 4:1–13)

4 ¹*Hear this word, you cows of Bashan*
   who are in Mount Samaria
Who oppress the poor
   who crush the needy
Who say to their husbands
   "Bring and we will drink!"
²*Lord Yahweh has sworn by his holiness*
   for behold the days are coming upon you
When he will take you away with hooks
   yes, the last of you with fishhooks
³*And you shall go out through the breaches*
   each one in front of her
      and you shall be thrown into Harmon
            oracle of Yahweh.

⁴*Come to Bethel and transgress*
   to Gilgal and multiply transgression
And bring your sacrifices in the morning
   your tithes every three days

5 And make a thank offering of leavened bread
   and proclaim freewill offerings, publish them
 For so you love it, O children of Israel!
         oracle of Lord Yahweh.

6 And also I, I gave you
   cleanness of teeth in all your cities
 And a lack of bread in all your places
   yet you did not return to me
         oracle of Yahweh.

7 And also I, I withheld the rain from you
   when there were yet three months to the harvest
 And I would send rain on one city
   and on another city I would not send rain
 One portion would be rained upon
   and the portion on which it did not rain withered
8 So two or three cities went in search to one city
   to drink water, and were not satisfied
     yet you did not return to me
             oracle of Yahweh.

9 I struck you with blight and with mildew
   I laid waste your gardens and your vineyards
 Your fig trees and your olive trees the locust devoured
   yet you did not return to me
         oracle of Yahweh.

10 I sent against you a pestilence after the manner of Egypt
   I killed with the sword your young men with your captured
   horses
 And I made the stench of your camp go up into your nostrils
   yet you did not return to me
             oracle of Yahweh.

^{11}*I overthrew some of you*
> *as when God overthrew Sodom and Gomorrah*
> *And you were as a stick plucked from the burning*
> > *yet you did not return to me*
> > > > *oracle of Yahweh.*

^{12}*Therefore thus I will do to you, O Israel*
> *because of this I will do to you*
> > *prepare to meet your God, O Israel!*
^{13}*For behold, the one who forms the mountains*
> *and creates the wind*
> > *and reveals to a person his thoughts*
> *Who makes the dawn darkness*
> > *and treads on the heights of the earth*
> > *Yahweh God of hosts is his name.*

THESE VERSES CONTAIN A series of oracles, the first two focusing on Samaria (4:1–3) and the Bethel sanctuary (4:4–5), which repeats the sequence of Samaria and Bethel oracles in 3:9–12 and 3:13–15. The five oracles in 4:6–11, leading up to the climactic oracle in 4:12–13, recall past judgments and announce a coming judgment upon Israel, then lifting high the name of Yahweh, God of hosts. We see again how Amos sets up a climactic oracle by using other oracles as a foil (cf. 1:3–2:16; 3:3–8).

HEAR THIS WORD, YOU COWS OF BASHAN (AMOS 4:1–3)

Amos in this oracle addresses the "cows of Bashan," who are pampered, well-fed women living in Samaria. Bashan was situated in the Transjordanian highlands that extended from Mount Hermon in the north (Deut 3:10; Josh 12:4–5) to the

Yarmuk River in the south. It was mountainous country (Ps 68:15), known for its rich pasture, choice livestock (Deut 32:14; Ps 22:12; Mic 7:14), and stands of oak trees (Isa 2:13; Ezek 27:6). Samaria, capital of Northern Israel, is not much of a mountain, but it does sit atop a hill. These women are oppressing the poor and needy (2:6–7), insisting that their husbands (Hebrew: "lords") bring them more wine to drink. The imperative (v. 1) is emphatic. Amos declares woe on the same in 6:4–6, seen there as lying on beds of ivory, eating lamb and tender beef, singing psalms of David, drinking wine in bowls, and rubbing themselves with the finest of oils, but caring nothing about a nation going to ruin. Samaria had ivory, as excavations have shown. Over five hundred ivory fragments from the ninth and eighth centuries BC have been found in Samaria. Palaces and houses of the wealthy had walls (wood paneling) and furniture decorated with inlaid ivory (Amos 3:15; 1 Kgs 22:39). In 3:9–10 Amos calls for neighboring nations to assemble on Mount Samaria and see the oppressions going on there. He says violence and robbery are being stored up in strongholds of evildoers. The term "violence," which means "lawlessness," turns up often in the Psalms (Pss 7:16; 11:5; 18:48; 25:19; 27:12; 35:11).

Amos cites oppression in Mount Samaria again in 3:9. Hosea saw it going on in the marketplace (Hos 12:7). Micah saw oppression in Jerusalem (Mic 2:2). Prov 31:20 says the good woman opens her hand to the poor and needy. It also says, "Those who oppress the poor insult their Maker, but those who are kind to the needy honor him" (Prov 14:31). Justice and benevolence to the vulnerable and disadvantaged, namely, the poor, needy, orphan, widow, sojourner, and pensioned Levite, are mandated in Deuteronomy (Deut 10:18; cf. Exod 22:21–22), where one not heeding this command can look forward to being "oppressed" and "crushed" by an enemy (Deut 28:33; cf. Exod 22:23–24). Yahweh cares for these people (Hos 14:3; Pss 10:14, 18; 68:5–6; 146:9).

Well, Lord Yahweh swears by his holiness that a day of reckoning awaits the affluent of Samaria (Amos 4:2). Yahweh's name is holy (cf. Matt 6:9), and here he swears by it. Only Yahweh can swear by his own name. The Hebrew contains a wordplay in "sworn" and "we will drink" (cf. Amos 4:1). The stereotypical "behold the days are coming" occurs elsewhere in Amos (8:11; 9:13), also in Jeremiah (Jer 7:32; 9:25; 16:14; etc.). Yahweh will take away these rank evildoers with hooks, the last of them with fishhooks (cf. Hab 1:14–15; Jer 16:16; Eccl 9:12). This is Amos's view of a remnant (cf. 3:12). Reference could be to people being led away with hooks in their noses, or to dead bodies being dragged away with hooks like animal carcasses to the refuse heap. Both could be envisioned. People able to walk will exit through breaches in the city wall, captive women going in single file. Their destination in Harmon is unknown; the term appears nowhere else in the OT. The Vulgate emends to "Hermon," which is north of Bashan and would tie in with v. 1. Surviving women will probably be going into exile.

COME TO BETHEL AND TRANSGRESS (AMOS 4:4–5)

This second oracle begins with an ironic "Come to Bethel and transgress." Calling one to do something of which one disapproves is *epitrope* in the Greek rhetorical handbooks (Latin: *permissio*). This is the first of seven imperatives censuring the Bethel sanctuary, paganized as it was by an idolatrous calf and other debased activities going on (3:14; 5:5; cf. 1 Kgs 12:28–30). Amos himself visited Bethel (7:10–13).

Hosea also heaps scorn on the idolatrous calves in North Israel (Hos 8:4–6; 13:2).

Amos invites people to also visit the sanctuary at Gilgal, an old worship site located in the Jordan Valley near Jericho (Josh 4:19–20; 1 Sam 7:16). Like Bethel it had fallen into disrepute because of what was going on there (Hos 9:15; 12:11). Both Amos and Hosea censure worship at Gilgal (Amos 5:5; Hos 4:15). Amos says that if people want they can bring sacrifices in the morning and tithes every three days to Gilgal! More irony in the urgency: worshipers can go there early and often. On the expression "in the morning," see Exod 34:2; Ps 30:5; Jer 21:11. A tithe (= 10 percent) was to be surrendered from all of one's agricultural produce: i.e., grain, wine, oil, and any other produce whose growth was from the soil (*m. Ma'aś* 1:1). Later legislation also called for a tithe of one's herds and flocks (Lev 27:32). Deuteronomy called for tithes at the central sanctuary every three years (Deut 14:28), although some paid them yearly (Deut 14:22). Reforms of both Hezekiah and Josiah required worship at a central sanctuary because syncretistic practices had taken over the local sanctuaries, bringing Yahweh worship into grave danger (Deut 12:5–6). Local sanctuaries at some point were closed down. Amos and other eighth-century prophets expressed strong displeasure of sacrifices and worship generally for two reasons: (1) Local sanctuaries had become paganized like the Canaanite cultic sites abolished earlier (Hos 8:11–13; 9:1–4; 10:1; 13:2), and (2) moral, ethical, and proper internal dispositions were being violated (Amos 5:21–24; Hos 6:6; Mic 6:6–8; Isa 1:10–17).

A thank offering was to be an offering of unleavened bread (Lev 7:12–15). Freewill offerings were also thank offerings, made when the worshiper was simply giving thanks for God's goodness (Exod 35:29; Ps 54:6). To publish them would mean to be ostentatious about making them (cf. Matt 6:2; 23:5). Such behavior made the offering ineffectual. More irony—even sarcasm—in Amos's concluding words, "For so you love it, O children of Israel!" (4:5; cf. Jer 5:31).

PREPARE TO MEET YOUR GOD, O ISRAEL! (AMOS 4:6–13)

In the following litany of oracles Yahweh reminds Israel about prior calamities not having had any effect. In each case people did not return to him. Yahweh gave them cleanness of teeth and a lack of bread in cities and elsewhere; people lacked food because of drought and famine, cited next (vv. 7–8). Note another emphatic "I" in the divine speech. But people did not return, where the Hebrew verb can also be translated "repent." Repentance is a key theme in the prophets (Hos 2:7; 3:5; 5:4; 6:1; 14:1–2; Joel 2:12–13; Jer 3:1–4:2; 8:4–5; etc.). But sometimes punishment does no good (cf. Deut 21:18). Sin goes deep, and even Yahweh cannot correct, winnow, or refine his people (Jer 2:30; 5:3; 6:27–30; 15:5–9). Jeremiah discovered in sin an irreversible quality where people were unable to change their evil behavior (Jer 8:4–7; 13:23). The rabbis said later that only God can help them make a change.

Yahweh says he withheld rain when there were yet three months to harvest (Amos 4:7). Another emphatic "I." Reference here is to the latter rains of March and April, which are more gentle than the early rains of winter. First comes the barley harvest, then in May and June the harvest of wheat. One city would get rain; another not; one portion of land would be rained upon, another portion not, so everything withered (Amos 4:7). Rain comes from Yahweh (Deut 28:12; Jer 5:24; 14:22) but is withheld when covenant people fail to obey the commandments (Deut 11:13–17;

28:23–24). For a connection in the OT between sin and a lack of rain, see 1 Kgs 8:35–36; 17:1—18:46; Jer 3:2–3; 5:24–25; 12:4. Treaties of the ANE also contain curses of drought for treaty violation. Two or three cities would go to one city in search of water, but not get enough to drink (Amos 4:8). Cities mean people living in the cities. Samaria was especially dependent upon rain because it had no natural water supply; all the rain had to be preserved in cisterns. A drought should have resulted in prayer and repentance (Jer 14:1–9), but Israel did neither.

Yahweh struck his people with blight and mildew, more covenant curses (Amos 4:9; Deut 28:22). Blight is smut (black spots) on field crops, also plant damage in gardens and vineyards and on fig and olive trees, commonly caused by the hot east wind off the desert (Gen 41:6, 23, 27; Hos 13:15). Mildew is a destructive growth of minute fungi on plants, leaving a white or pale-yellow coating. Solomon in his prayer of dedication for the temple called upon Yahweh to answer prayers of people when these or other like calamities arose (1 Kgs 8:37–40). But Amos assumes people do not pray (cf. Hag 2:17). Locusts devoured the olive and fig trees (Joel 1:4–7), another covenant curse (Deut 28:38).

Yahweh also sent a pestilence after the manner of Egypt (Amos 4:10), where "pestilence" means death (Deut 28:21). The divine word is now cutting deep. It seems Yahweh has done to Israel what he did to the Egyptians, for a great pestilence preceded the exodus (Exod 9:3). Yahweh threatened to bring it upon Israel in the wilderness (Num 14:12), and in the Song of Moses Yahweh again promised famine, pestilence, sword, and other calamities in response to Israel's idolatry (Deut 32:24–25). They came. Jeremiah later preached without letup about a pestilence destined to come upon Judah, coining the triad, "sword, famine, and pestilence" (Jer 14:12; 18:21; 21:6–7, 9; 32:24, 36; etc.).

Yahweh says he also killed Israel's young men and their captured horses, the stench of the unburied filling the camp (Amos 4:10; Isa 34:3; Joel 2:20). Kings of Samaria had horses and chariots, some probably captured from the Syrians (2 Kgs 13:7; Ezek 23:6). At the Red Sea it was Egyptian young men and their horses plunging into the depths like a stone (Exod 15:1–10). During the US Civil War, after the Battle of Gettysburg, July 1–3, 1863, the Peach Orchard was strewn with dead horses, the stench of which is said to have lasted for days and weeks.

In Amos 4:11 Yahweh says he overthrew some in Israel like when he overthrew Sodom and Gomorrah (Gen 18–19), an event firmly implanted in Israel's collective memory, and recalled often by the prophets (Isa 1:9; 3:9; 13:19; Hos 11:8; Zeph 2:9; Jer 5:1–8; 20:16; 23:14; 49:18; 50:40; Ezek 16:46–52). In this calamity, whatever it was, which may also have been the worst, those saved were a stick pulled from a blazing fire—like Lot and his family. But the survivors did not return to Yahweh.

Israel had experienced judgment in the past, but because punishments did no good, the final oracle gives a climactic word from Yahweh: "Prepare to meet your God, O Israel!" (Amos 4:12). The term "meet" is deliberately neutral so the audience can decide what will happen next. Yahweh has run out of patience (7:1–9). The oracle concludes with a doxology lifting up Israel's all-powerful God. This is another mark of Amos's prophecies (5:8–9; 9:5–6), where, after sweeping judgments and impassioned denunciations, a strong word follows, extolling the God of creation and his power over creation (cf. Deut 10:14; Jer 10:16 [51:19]; 33:2; Job 38:1–41).

Yahweh is the one who forms the mountains and creates the winds (Job 38:24; Pss 65:6; 95:4). Yahweh also reveals to a person his thoughts (Jer 33:3). He makes the dawn darkness (Amos 8:5; Joel 2:2), and treads on the heights of the earth. The oracle concludes with a climactic "Yahweh God of hosts is his name" (Amos 4:13), another signature of this prophet (5:8; 9:6), although climactic statements naming Yahweh appear often in the OT (Exod 15:3; Deut 32:3; Hos 12:5), especially in Jeremiah and Second Isaiah (Jer 10:16 [51:19]; 31:35; 33:2; Isa 47:4; 48:2; 51:15; 54:5).

REFLECTION

1. Who today are the "cows of Bashan," with husbands giving them too much to drink? To what extent does extravagant living go hand in hand with oppression of the poor and needy?

2. How do you feel about Amos's characterization of worship as it was being carried on? Are you willing to hear someone censure worship today, and if so, why and in what way?

3. Do we view natural calamities such as the Dutch elm disease in the Midwest; the HIV crisis; hurricanes flooding New Orleans, Houston, and other Gulf cities; wildfires in California and the Pacific Northwest; and most recently the worldwide COVID-19 pandemic as judgments of God? Why, or why not?

4. Can we still affirm a God of creation with all the modern scientific explanations now available about how the created order came into being? If so, how do we combine the two?

5

"SEEK YAHWEH AND LIVE" (AMOS 5:1-15)

5 ¹*Hear this word that I lift up over you in lamentation,*
   O house of Israel:
   ²*Fallen, not to rise again*
      is virgin Israel
   Forsaken on her land
      none is there to raise her up
   ³*For thus said Lord Yahweh:*
   The city that marched out a thousand
      shall have a hundred remaining
   And that which marched out a hundred
      shall have ten remaining
         to the house of Israel.

   ⁴*For thus said Yahweh to the house of Israel:*
   Seek me and live
      ⁵*but do not seek Bethel*
   And Gilgal do not enter
      or Beersheba cross not over

"Seek Yahweh and Live" (Amos 5:1–15)

For Gilgal shall surely go into exile
and Bethel shall come to nothing
6Seek Yahweh and live
lest he rush like fire O house of Joseph
and it consume with none to extinguish for Bethel
7Those who turn justice to wormwood
and righteousness to the earth, you cast down
8The one who made the Pleiades and Orion
and who turns into the morning deep darkness
and darkens the day to night
Who calls for the waters of the sea
and pours them out on the surface of the earth
Yahweh is his name.
9Who makes destruction flash out upon the strong
so that destruction comes upon the fortress.

10They hate the one who reproves in the gate
and the one who speaks truth they abhor
11Therefore because you trample on the poor
and take from them taxes of grain
Houses of hewn stone you have built
but you shall not live in them
Pleasant vineyards you have planted
but you shall not drink their wine
12Indeed I know how many are your transgressions
and how great are your sins
Afflicting the righteous, taking a bribe
and turning aside the needy in the gate
13Therefore the prudent will keep silent in such a time
for it is an evil time
14Seek good and not evil
in order that you may live
And so Yahweh God of hosts will be with you
as you have said

> [15]Hate evil and love good
>   and establish justice in the gate
> Perhaps Yahweh God of hosts will be gracious
>   O remnant of Joseph.

THE PRESENT VERSES CONTAIN three oracles delimited by section markings in the Hebrew Bible at the end of vv. 3, 8, and 15. Verse 9 is an add-on to the second oracle, which originally ended with the climactic naming of Yahweh. The first oracle is a lament over Israel; the second an admonition to seek Yahweh and live, concluding with a doxology; and the third an indictment for injustice in the city gate followed by judgment and a concluding admonition to seek good and not evil.

FALLEN, NOT TO RISE AGAIN, IS VIRGIN ISRAEL (AMOS 5:1–3)

Here at the beginning Yahweh or Amos is making a lament over Israel, who ironically is called a "virgin." A virgin is a maiden of marriageable age (Judg 11:34–40; Jer 2:32), and even metaphorically Israel is not that (cf. Jer 14:17; 18:13; 31:4, 21). The editorial introduction begins with "Hear," similar to 3:1. The "Hear (this)" beginnings in 4:1 and 8:4 are genuine. The verses here are in a falling (3:2) rhythm, called the *qina*, common for laments. People have died, and professional mourning women will be called in to help people begin their wailing (5:16b; Jer 9:17–22). In 5:16–17 Yahweh speaks of wailing to be heard in city streets and squares, also by farmers in their fields and vineyards. The book of Lamentations is a collection of laments made after Jerusalem's fall in 587 BC.

Israel has fallen, not to rise again. No one is there to raise her up; she finds herself alone in her greatest hour of need (Amos 5:2; cf. Jer 15:5; Lam 1:1–2, 17, 21). After the lament comes a divine oracle. Yahweh says out of one city will march a thousand, but only one hundred will be left; out of another city will march a hundred, but only ten will be left. Israel's fighting force will be 90 percent decimated (Amos 5:3).

SEEK YAHWEH AND LIVE (AMOS 5:4–9)

Now comes an admonition, with Yahweh in a divine word telling how life ought to be lived. These are some of Amos's most hopeful words, and it sounds almost as if he is calling for reform. The oracle contains an expanded messenger formula serving as introduction. Up until the doxology the oracle is structured into a chiasmus: "Seek me and live : Bethel : Gilgal : Beersheba : Gilgal : Bethel : Seek Yahweh and live." Another rhetorical flourish from the sheep breeder of Tekoa.

The way to live is to seek Yahweh—seek him with all one's heart (Deut 4:29; Jer 29:13). The wise seek after God (Pss 14:2; 53:2). Everyone should seek Yahweh while he may be found (Isa 55:6–7). Deuteronomy teaches that life comes in obeying Yahweh's commandments (Deut 4:1; 8:1; 30:15–20; 32:46–47). In the OT seeking Yahweh can mean seeking him in worship (Deut 12:5; Ps 27:4), but here people are told not to do their seeking at the sanctuaries of Bethel, Gilgal, or Beersheba. Bethel is censured in Amos 3:14, and both Bethel and Gilgal in 4:4. Hosea too says not to go to Gilgal or Beth-aven, which is Bethel called "House of Wickedness" (Hos 4:15; 5:8; 10:5). Beersheba is a southern sanctuary in Judah about fifty miles south southwest of

Jerusalem (8:14). People from the north might cross over to worship there (Amos 8:14). The verse in Hebrew is full of wordplays.

Amos, now the speaker, says, "Seek Yahweh and live" (5:6). Why? Otherwise Yahweh will rush like a fire upon the house of Joseph. Joseph is the ancestor of the Ephraim and Manasseh tribes, in Amos meaning Northern Israel (5:15; 6:6). The fire will devour Bethel (cf. 2 Kgs 23:15). Yahweh's wrath can burn with great intensity such that no one can quench it (Deut 32:22; 2 Kgs 22:17; Jer 4:4; 7:20; 21:12). Amos says that those turning justice to wormwood and righteousness to the earth Yahweh will cast down (5:7). Another chiasmus in the Hebrew: "those who turn : to wormwood : justice : and righteousness : to the earth : you cast down." In 6:12 Amos says people have turned justice into poison and the fruit of righteousness into wormwood. In the OT justice and righteousness go together (Isa 1:21; 5:7; Jer 22:3; Pss 72:1–2; 89:14). Wormwood is absinthe, a bitter plant used for making a potent alcoholic drink. In the OT it is a metaphor for suffering and death (Lam 3:19; Jer 9:15; 23:15). The process will be reversed for Israel when justice rolls down like waters (5:24).

What follows is another of Amos's hymnic praises to Yahweh. Yahweh made Pleiades and Orion (Job 9:9; 38:31), two groups of stars associated with the New Year and the change from winter to summer. Pleiades is a constellation of seven stars, Orion a bright constellation near Pleiades. Yahweh turns deep darkness into morning (Amos 4:13; Job 12:22), and darkens the day to night (Exod 10:21–22; Pss 104:20; 105:28). Yahweh calls for waters of the sea, pouring them out on the surface of the earth. Sounds like Yahweh is the one bringing hurricanes. The oracle concludes with another climactic "Yahweh is his name" (4:13; 9:6). The add-on v. 9 has Yahweh making destruction flash upon the strong and the fortress.

THEY HATE ONE WHO REPROVES IN THE GATE (AMOS 5:10–15)

The city gate is where court is held and the elders sit assembled (Deut 21:19; 22:15; 25:7; Ruth 4:1–2). What is happening is that those prosecuting evildoers are hated for speaking out against them. Elders and others present may not always themselves be speaking the truth, but what they will not hear is someone who does speak the truth (Amos 5:10). Honest testimony must be heard in the city gate. The seventh commandment forbids false witness against a neighbor, which is perjury (Exod 20:16; Deut 5:20), with Deuteronomy saying that malicious witnesses will be punished according to the *lex talionis* (Deut 19:16–21). Miscarriages of justice are deplored also by Isaiah (Isa 29:21).

Yahweh therefore has a word to those who trample the poor and collect too much tax on grain (Amos 2:7; 8:4–6). These are wealthy landlords taking an excessive share of produce from those farming the land. They have built houses of hewn stone but will not live in them; they have planted pleasant vineyards but will not drink their wine (5:11). Excavations at Samaria have turned up courses of hewn stone when Phoenician craftsmen were brought in to do the work. In wartime vineyards are planted and others eat the fruit (Deut 20:6; Jer 5:17). For more futility curses, see Mic 6:14–15. These reverse Yahweh's goodness from when Israel came into the land (Deut 6:10–11). Israel was warned about curses such as these in Deuteronomy (Deut 28:30–34), also by other prophets (Zeph 1:13; Jer 5:17; 6:12; 8:10). Later, when Jerusalem and all Judah reaped the bitter fruit of its covenant disregard, these curses and others actually came to pass (Lam 5:1–9).

Yahweh knows how many are Israel's transgressions (Amos 2:6–8, 12). Cited here are afflicting the righteous, taking a bribe, and turning aside the needy in the gate (5:12). Justice must not be perverted (Deut 16:19), and all of these acts are perversions of justice. Judges were solemnly admonished to render righteous judgment and not to take bribes (Exod 23:8; Deut 16:18–19; Num 35:31). A curse was laid upon anyone taking a bribe (Deut 27:25). Yahweh will not be bribed (Deut 10:17). Amos deplored oppression of the righteous and the needy in 2:6. Two actions of the hand are here being censured: (1) having an open hand to accept bribes and (2) refusing with outstretched hand the needy in the gate. Amos again resorts to bitter irony, saying that the prudent out of fear of reprisal will keep silent in such a time, for it is an evil time (v. 13). A bit of wisdom mixed in with his prophetic message. We know this is irony because Amos himself is not keeping silent about such evils.

Amos then turns to admonition such as we heard in vv. 4–6. Wisdom of a different sort: people are told to seek a moral and ethical life. Isaiah and Jeremiah also told people to turn things around (Isa 1:16–17; Jer 6:16). Amos says here to seek good and not evil in order that people may live. Yahweh God of hosts will then be with them as promised (5:14). How are people to go about seeking good? Answer: By hating evil and loving good, by establishing justice in the gate, the very things not currently being done (vv. 10–11). These words find an echo in the NT (Rom 12:9; 3 John 11). Amos concludes by saying that perhaps Yahweh will be gracious, O remnant of Joseph (v. 15)—more irony, because Amos is not sure it will happen. Speaking of a remnant is a return to the same in v. 3.

REFLECTION

1. The OT teaches that God "found" Israel (Deut 32:10; Hos 9:10), and in the NT Jesus says people are lost sheep needing to be "found" (Luke 15:3–7). Should we also have to seek God, and if so, how do we do it? Have a look at Isa 55:6 and Matt 7:7.

2. How are people today turning justice to wormwood?

3. Is justice only defending the poor and those with no advocate and not prosecuting evildoers? Some highly paid defense lawyers have never prosecuted a case.

4. What is the difference between bribing and simply giving a gift?

6

"LET JUSTICE ROLL DOWN LIKE WATERS" (AMOS 5:18-24)

5 18Woe to those who desire the day of Yahweh
    why would you want the day of Yahweh?
      it is darkness, not light
  19As if a man fled from a lion
    and a bear met him
  Or entered the house and rested the hand against the wall
    and a snake bit him
  20Is not the day of Yahweh darkness and not light
    and gloom, with no brightness in it?

  21I hate, I despise your festivals
    and I take no delight in your solemn assemblies
  22Even though you offer me your burnt offerings and grain offerings
    I will not accept them

> And the peace offerings of your fatted animals
>   I will not look upon
> 23 Take away from me the noise of your songs
>   and to the melody of your harps I will not listen
> 24 But let justice roll down like waters
>   and righteousness like an everflowing stream.

THE PRESENT VERSES APPEAR to combine two originally brief oracles: 5:18–20, announcing the "day of Yahweh," and 5:21–24, delivering strong words about worship generally, with the prose in 5:25–27 being a later add-on questioning sacrifices and offerings and predicting that Israel will take her idols with her into exile. The add-on verses end with a climactic naming of Yahweh God of hosts. All of 5:18–27 is delimited as a single unit by section markings in the Hebrew Bible.

WOE TO THOSE WHO DESIRE THE DAY OF YAHWEH (AMOS 5:18–20)

Amos in this oracle speaks a woe on people who look forward to the "day of Yahweh." "Woe" is a prophetic invective coming close to a curse, heard elsewhere from Amos in 6:1, and spoken also by Hosea (Hos 7:13; 9:12), Micah (Mic 2:1), Isaiah (Isa 1:4; 5:8–25), and other prophets (Nah 3:1; Hab 2:6–19; Zeph 2:5; 3:1; Jer 13:27; 22:13; 23:1; Ezek 13:3, 18). The "day of Yahweh" is believed to be an old holy war idea where the expectation was that Yahweh on a given day would bring Israel victory over its enemies (Josh 8:25; 10:12–14, 28, 32). Nevertheless, this is the first occurrence of the expression in the OT, and some think Amos may have coined it. Amos otherwise simply refers to "the (evil) day" (3:14; 6:3) or "that day" (2:16; 8:3, 9, 13). For the idea elsewhere in the prophets, see Isa 13:6–21; 34:8–17; Zeph 1:7–18; 2:2–3; 3:8, 11–20; Joel 1:15.

Amos asks why people would desire the day of Yahweh. No doubt for the same reason they have always desired it. But Amos has a surprise: It will be darkness, not light (5:18). The return to darkness routinely describes Yahweh's day of judgment (Amos 8:9; Isa 13:10; Joel 2:2; Zeph 1:15; Jer 13:16), a day when no one will escape (Amos 9:1–4). The images, deriving from the hunt, speak for themselves (cf. Isa 24:18; Jer 16:16; 48:44). On Yahweh's judgment being compared to the attack of wild animals, see Deut 32:24; Hos 13:7–8; Jer 5:6. Amos has Yahweh commanding the sea serpent to bite fleeing evildoers in 9:3. In Joel 1:4 Yahweh's judgment is a locust parade. Amos concludes his oracle by asking his hearers if what he announced at the beginning was not in fact on the horizon.

LET JUSTICE ROLL DOWN LIKE WATERS (AMOS 5:21–24)

Here Yahweh speaks strong condemnation on Israel's festivals, solemn assemblies, and other worship activities. Festivals were the yearly pilgrim feasts of Passover, Weeks (Pentecost), and Booths, where every Israelite man had to appear with gifts in hand (Exod 23:14–17; 34:18–23; Deut 16:1–17). Entire households, the sojourner, orphan, and widow, and also the Levite in town were invited to make the pilgrimage with him. Festivals carried on at Yahweh's sanctuary were times of joyful celebration (Deut 12:7, 12, 18; 16:11, 14). There was a special joy at harvest time (Isa 9:3; Ruth 2–3; Ps 126:5–6). But on the day of Yahweh, feasts will be turned into mourning, grievous mourning like the mourning for an only son (cf. Jer 6:26; Zech 12:10). Sackcloth will be on all loins and baldness on every head

(Amos 8:10). Yahweh usually delighted in the solemn assemblies, which would be convened at the annual feasts (Deut 16:8; 31:10–13), but not now. Isaiah condemns the same occurring in Judah (Isa 1:11–15).

At the annual festivals, also at other times, burnt offerings and grain offerings were made to Yahweh. Burnt offerings, the most important, were sacrifices in which the entire animal was consumed on the altar (Lev 1). Grain offerings were originally any gifts offered to Yahweh or for the benefit of the worshiper but later denoted an offering to Yahweh consisting of grain such as flour, roasted kernels, unleavened bread, and the like (Lev 2). Peace or well-being offerings were animal offerings showing friendship to Yahweh (Lev 3). Smoke from these offerings pleased Yahweh (Lev 3:5; cf. Gen 8:21). In peace offerings only part of the victim was consumed on the altar; a portion went to the priest, and the remainder was eaten by the worshiper and his friends. Offerings were judged acceptable or unacceptable by the priest (Lev 1:4; 7:18; 19:5–7; 22:17–29). But now Yahweh will not pay heed to any of them (cf. Gen 4:4–5). Yahweh is disavowing even offerings of friendship (cf. Jer 3:4). Prophets generally are critical of sacrificial worship (Amos 4:4; Hos 6:6; 8:13; 9:4; Isa 1:11; Jer 6:20; 7:21–22).

Yahweh also hears people's songs as so much noise and will not listen to the sweet sounds of the harp (Ps 144:9). There are five books of psalms in the Psalter, and does not Yahweh want to hear any of them? Yahweh is otherwise pleased with music in worship, but not now. Amos also disparages the wealthy who sing idle songs to music of the harp (6:5). On the day of Yahweh palace songs will become wailings (5:16–17; 8:3).

Then in one of Amos's most memorable prophecies, Yahweh says: "But let justice roll down like waters, and righteousness like an everflowing stream" (5:24). An everflowing stream (Arabic: *wadi*) is a stream that becomes a virtual torrent in rainy season. It describes judgment in Isa 30:28 and Jer 47:2. Isaiah sees Yahweh bringing up the mighty waters of the Euphrates to pour as a flood into Judah (Isa 8:5–8).

But it seems in this oracle as if something has been left out, although it is not been left out in Amos's other preaching: Israel has not been practicing justice and righteousness—righteous people are being sold for silver and the needy for a pair of sandals; loose soil is tamped with heads of the poor; the afflicted are being pushed aside; father and son are having sex with the same girl; garments taken in pledge from the poor are not being returned at sundown; priests are drinking wine of those fined in the sanctuary (2:6–8); the wealthy in Samaria are oppressing the poor and crushing the needy (4:1); justice is not carried on in the city gate, with people there not willing to hear the truth; the poor are being trampled on; people are being overtaxed on their grain (5:10–11); the righteous are being afflicted; people are taking bribes; the needy are being turned aside in the gate (5:12). Justice and the fruit of righteousness have been turned into wormwood and poison, and righteousness to earth (5:7; 6:12).

Righteousness originally meant "straightness," being both a principle and a concrete act. For Amos righteousness was a principle; for Deuteronomy it was "doing the commandments" (Deut 6:25). Deuteronomy tells judges and officials, "Righteousness, righteousness, you shall pursue" (Deut 16:18–20). The Hebrew term for justice originally denoted a judgment determined by custom or precedent; later it came to mean the proper administration of law in society. Justice was equitable and impartial action in conformity with what was legally and morally right, where such was defined ultimately by stipulations of the Sinai covenant; it was giving to each person what they deserved. It was not simply aiding the oppressed but also bringing judgment to the oppressor. Justice consisted of rendering right and fair decisions of punishment and vindication. The problem here was that Israel was not practicing righteousness and justice, so Yahweh will bring justice and righteousness to Israel.

REFLECTION

1. What does the "day of the Lord" mean today? Or does it have more than one meaning?

2. How would you feel if someone came along and said that the Lord hated your church suppers or Christmas celebrations, or did not want your tithes and offerings?

3. Might the Lord not want to hear songs sung in church or a Christmas oratorio? Why, or why not?

4. Have you thought of righteousness as meaning "straight"—expressed in expressions such as "straight talk" or "being straight arrow"? What about people who are themselves "straight"?

7

"I SAW THE LORD STATIONED UPON THE ALTAR" (AMOS 9:1-6)

9 ¹*I saw the Lord stationed upon the altar, and he said:*
  Strike the capital and shake the thresholds
 And break them off on the head of all of them
   and what is left of them I will kill with the sword
 And the one of them that flees shall not flee away
   and the one of them that escapes shall not escape
 ²*If they dig into Sheol*
  from there my hand shall take them
 And if they climb up to heaven
  from there I will bring them down
 ³*And if they hide themselves on the top of Carmel*
  from there I will search out and take them
 And if they are concealed from my sight in the bottom of the sea
  from there I will command the sea-serpent and it shall bite them

4*And if they go into captivity before their enemies*
  from there I will command the sword and it shall kill
  them
 And I will fix my eyes upon them
  for evil and not for good
5*Yes Lord Yahweh of hosts*
 The one who touches the earth and it melts
  and all who dwell in it mourn
 And all of it rises like the Nile
  and sinks like the Nile of Egypt
6*The one who builds his upper chambers in the heaven*
  and establishes his vault upon the earth
 The one who calls for the waters of the sea
  and pours them out upon the surface of the earth
  Yahweh is his name.

THE PRESENT VERSES APPEAR to be a single oracle concluding with another of Amos's doxologies. The verses are not delimited at the lower end by a section in the Hebrew Bible, but the doxology concludes with a climactic "Yahweh is his name."

THE LORD STATIONED UPON THE ALTAR (AMOS 9:1–6)

Amos here reports seeing the Lord stationed upon the altar, not beside the altar, as the RSV and NRSV have it. The RSV and NRSV also have LORD, i.e., Yahweh, which is not right, since the Hebrew has "Lord" (KJV; cf. 8:1), probably to dispel any idea of Amos actually having seen Yahweh. No one can see Yahweh. This is a vision, similar to other visions reported by Amos (7:1–9; 8:1). Yahweh in the OT does not allow his face to be seen, for which reason Moses can only catch a glimpse of his back as he passes by (Exod 33:20–23). Isaiah, too, in his vision in the temple, can only see the hem of Yahweh's robe as he sits upon his throne (Isa 6:1). Israelite religion was aniconic, disallowing idols, because at Sinai revelation came in hearing, not in seeing (Deut 4:12).

The Lord commands that the ornamental capitals atop the pillars of Israel's sanctuary be struck and the thresholds shaken. Pieces of the former are seen breaking off on the heads of everyone. Any who survive will be killed with the sword (Amos 9:1). Is this the sanctuary at Bethel, which Amos says is destined for destruction (3:14; 7:9)? Josiah later destroyed the altar at Bethel (2 Kgs 23:15). The Lord, in any case, is going to do at this sanctuary what Samson did at a sanctuary of the Philistines—only Samson stood between pillars to bring the house down (Judg 16:23–31). A great number were killed. But the Philistines got their revenge by destroying Israel's first sanctuary at Shiloh (1 Sam 4:10–11), which may also be in the back of Amos's mind. The memory of this disaster was so painful that it went unmentioned in Israel's history (1 Sam 4:10–11). But Jeremiah mentioned it in one of his temple oracles (Jer 7:13–14; 26:4–6; cf. Ps 78:60).

Yahweh says not everyone will be killed when his sanctuary tumbles. Some will flee, but they will not escape. Some will dig into Sheol, the place of the dead in the depths of the earth, but Yahweh will take them from there. Should some climb to highest heaven, Yahweh will bring them down (Amos 9:2). Some may try to hide in forested Mount Carmel, but Yahweh will search them out and capture them. Should some try to conceal themselves at the bottom of the sea, Yahweh will command his sea serpent to bite them (v. 3). Some may be taken by an enemy into exile, but even there Yahweh's sword will find them (v. 4). The enemy here would be the Assyrians, which Amos never mentions (against the RSV in 3:9). The sword is almost personified, but acting under Yahweh's command (cf. Hos 11:6; Jer 47:6–7; 49:37; 50:35–37; Ezek 14:17).

Yahweh has his eyes on people for evil, not for good (Amos 9:4, 8; cf. Jer 21:10; 39:16; 44:27). There is no way to flee from Israel's God (Amos 2:14–15; 5:18–19). Yahweh is everywhere present in his creation, also everywhere there to give protective care (Ps 139:7–12; 2 Sam 22:2–20 = Ps 18:2–19). Even heaven and highest heaven cannot contain Yahweh (1 Kgs 8:27). This passage, like Amos's survey of the nations of the world in 1:3—2:16 shows how Hebrew rhetoric strives after totality.

The oracle concludes with a doxology extolling Israel's God of creation. Yahweh's touching of the earth and its melting may refer to a flood (Amos 5:8; 9:6). The rise and fall of the Nile are cited for comparison (8:8). Yahweh's dwelling is in heaven (Deut 26:15). In the OT the heaven or sky is thought to be a solid firmament in the shape of an inverted bowl, or vault, its base resting on the earth. The architecture of Eastern churches with their dome roofs, e.g., the Hagia Sophia in Istanbul, reflect this ancient worldview. Here it appears as if Yahweh's chambers are above the vault. Yahweh's call for sea waters to be poured out on the earth will mean a flood—a major flood. The doxology ends with another climactic "Yahweh is his name" (4:13; 5:8).

REFLECTION

1. Does Amos's vision anticipate two predictions of the destruction of the Jerusalem temple by Jeremiah and Jesus? See Jer 7:14 and Matt 24:2.

2. Would you agree that there is no way to escape the all-searching eye and all-reaching hand of God?

3. The OT also contains the idiom of "fixing one's eyes on someone for good" (Jer 24:6; 39:12). In what way has the Lord fixed his eyes on you for good?

4. What sort of doxology extolling God might we create today based on our modern view of the created order?

HOSEA

8

"I WILL BRING HER INTO THE WILDERNESS" (HOS 2:2-15)

2 ²*Find fault with your mother, find fault—*
for she is not my wife
and I am not her husband–
That she remove her harlotry from her face
and her adultery from between her breasts
³*Lest I strip her naked*
and exhibit her as the day she was born
And constitute her as a wilderness
and make her as a land of drought
and kill her with thirst
⁴*And her children I will not pity*
for they are children of harlotry
⁵*For their mother has played the harlot*
she who conceived them acted shamefully
For she said, "I will go
after my lovers

They who give me my bread and my water
　my wool and my flax
　　my oil and my drink"
6Therefore behold I will hedge up
　your way with thorns
And I will build her a wall
　so her paths she cannot find
7And she shall pursue her lovers
　but she will not overtake them
Yes she shall seek them and not find
　then she will say, "I will go
And I will return to my first husband
　for it was better for me than now"
8And she did not know
　that I, I gave her
　　the grain and the new wine and the oil
And silver I lavished on her
　and gold they used for Baal
9Therefore I will take back
　my grain in its time
　　and my new wine in its season
And I will take away my wool and my flax
　which covered her nakedness
10And now I will uncover her genitals
　before the eyes of her lovers
　　and no man can rescue her from my hand
11And I will put an end to all her rejoicing
　her feast, her new moon, her sabbath
　　and all her appointed feasts
12And I will lay waste her vine and her fig tree
　of which she said
　"These are my hire
　which my lovers have given me"
And I will make them a thicket
　and beasts of the field will eat them

¹³*And I will punish her for the feast days of the Baals*
when she burned incense to them
And decked herself with her nose-ring and jewelry
and went after her lovers
and forgot me
oracle of Yahweh.

¹⁴*Therefore behold I will allure her*
and I will bring her into the wilderness
and I will speak to her heart
¹⁵*And I will give her her vineyards from there*
and the Valley of Achor as a door of hope
And there she shall answer as the days of her youth
and as the day she came up from the land of Egypt.

FIND FAULT WITH YOUR MOTHER, FIND FAULT! (HOS 2:2–13)

YAHWEH IN THIS FIRST oracle speaks to Israel as one addressing children about their unfaithful mother. The language is metaphorical. Jeremiah has Yahweh asking what wrong the "fathers" found in him, causing them to go far from him and become worthless (Jer 2:5). Here in Hosea the unfaithful mother and her children are Israel, an urban male elite in more recent sociological analysis; the aggrieved husband is Yahweh. The oracle begins on a sharp note with the verb translated "find fault" being a legal term that can also mean "accuse" or "bring a lawsuit." This is a solemn legal proceeding. Hosea does not employ the "Thus said Yahweh" messenger formula, beginning his oracle instead with Yahweh launching straightaway into an urgent plea. At the end is an "oracle of Yahweh" formula (2:13).

Yahweh says his covenant partner is no longer his wife, which is a strong statement, but does not imply divorce.

Reading on we see that Yahweh is only threatening divorce. To say that Israel is not his wife and he is not her husband has the same force as when Yahweh says "you are not my people" in Hos 1:9. Israel is still Yahweh's people, but right now she is not. The same is true about Israel being the wife: she is, but she is not. We are listening to emotive language from a hurt lover.

These children are to tell their mother to do away with her harlotry, which consists of loose living generally, and probably also participation in rituals of the Baal cults. Removing harlotry "from her face" could be a plea for her to abandon her obstinacy (Hos 4:16; cf. Jer 3:3), but "face" and "breasts" may also be interpreted literally, in which case the woman bears telltale marks or is wearing emblems—headbands, rings, necklaces, jewelry—on her body that identify her as a participant in Canaanite fertility rites. There were sexual rituals in Baal worship. Adultery would refer to women having sexual relations with someone other than her husband. Hosea's second wife is an adulteress (3:1). "Harlotry" is a looser term, referring to sexual relations an unmarried woman has with any man, which would include prostitution. All this and perhaps more is going on in Israel (4:2, 10, 12–15, 18; 5:3–4; 7:4; etc.). Because of these indiscretions Yahweh says he is ready to strip her naked (2:3), which is a threat of divorce, for when a husband divorces his wife he strips off her clothes since they belong to him (cf. Exod 21:10). She will thus be naked as in the day of her birth (Ezek 16:8). But as we have said, a divorce has not yet occurred; it is only threatened, and Yahweh means what he says.

Imagery now shifts to Israel's inhabited territory. Yahweh will make Israel's beautiful land into a wilderness: rain will not come, the land will be parched, and people will die of thirst (Hos 2:3b). Children will not be spared; being born of immoral parents, they must share their fate. Their mother has played the harlot and acted shamefully, intent on going after lovers whom she thinks have given her food and water, wool and flax, olive oil to make her skin soft and tender, and drink, which probably refers to wine and beer (2:5). These lovers are the Baals.

But Yahweh is going to put a stop to all this. He will put up a hedge with thorns so she cannot find the way to her lovers. She will continue to pursue, but not catch up to them. So what will she do? Well, she will decide that perhaps it was better with her first husband, and will return to him (2:7). Is her first husband Yahweh? Perhaps (6:1–3), but if so, what she still does not know is that Yahweh is the one who gave her grain, new wine, and olive oil (7:14; cf. Deut 7:13; 11:14). Yahweh also lavished on her the silver and gold she possesses. But the latter she used to overlay idols for the Baals (8:4–5; 13:2; cf. Isa 2:20; 30:22). So Yahweh vows now to take back the grain come harvest time (8:7; 9:2) and the wine made from grapes of the vineyard (9:2). He will take away the wool and flax she used to make beautiful clothes (2:9; cf. Prov 31:13) to cover her nakedness. Parts of the body always covered will now be seen by her lovers. There will be no one to come and rescue her from her indignity (5:14).

Shifting again to Israel's existence in the land she inhabits, Yahweh says he will put an end to all holidays and rejoicing: feasts, new moon celebrations, sabbath pleasures, and appointed feasts when people go to the sanctuaries on pilgrimage (Hos 9:5). Vines and fig trees will be laid waste because Israel thinks the gods of Canaan have given them to her. Yahweh calls them wages of a whore (9:1). Yahweh will transform all cultivated land into brush and overgrowth (9:6; 10:8), and wild animals will eat what remains of any grapes or figs. Wild animals suggest unwanted enemies.

This will be punishment for the feast days when Israel burned incense to the Baals—there were many local Baal cults who had feast days! This wayward woman is dressed up with a nose ring and other jewelry, chasing after lovers and forgetting Yahweh.

BEHOLD, I WILL ALLURE HER INTO THE WILDERNESS (HOS 2:14–15)

Then comes a second oracle in which Yahweh adopts a softer tone. No more indictments, threats of judgment, or complaints about Yahweh having been abandoned. But the "therefore" makes a connection with what precedes. Yahweh now decides to take Israel back into the wilderness and speak tenderly to her. The idea here, also in Hos 9:10–11; 11:1; 13:5, and expressed in the Song of Moses, and later in Jeremiah, is that the wilderness was the place of honeymoon when Israel was Yahweh's young bride (Deut 32:10–11; Jer 2:2–3), and Yahweh cared for her and she was devoted to him. Yahweh knew Israel in the wilderness (13:5). Things went bad when Israel settled in the land and adopted ways of the Moabites (9:10b) and Canaanites (11:2; 13:6). Passed over in silence is all of Israel's rebellion in the wilderness. But the wilderness now refers to exile, and talk of reconciliation will occur there. Yahweh decides he will again give Israel vineyards and make the Valley of Achor, where Achan suffered misfortune for hiding holy war booty (Josh 7:24–26), into a door of hope (2:15a). The hope is that Israel will then answer Yahweh as in the days of her youth, when Yahweh took her out of the land of Egypt (2:15b). Hosea makes many references to Yahweh's gracious deliverance of Israel from Egypt (11:1; 12:9, 13; 13:4). Israel answering God here may even allude to antiphonal singing like what occurred when Moses and Miriam sang the Song of the Sea following the deliverance from pursuing Egyptians (Exod 15:1, 21).

REFLECTION

1. What happens today in a marriage when the wife or husband proves unfaithful? Can things be salvaged so there is no divorce?

2. How does all this translate into calamities befalling a nation? Does not the land and people of the land suffer as a result?

3. What are modern counterparts to the merry feasts in honor of the Baals?

4. Do we know from whom the goodness of our land comes, or is this an outmoded biblical idea?

9

"NO FAITHFULNESS, STEADFAST LOVE, OR KNOWLEDGE OF GOD IN THE LAND" (HOS 4:1-19)

4 ¹*Hear the word of Yahweh, children of Israel*
for Yahweh has a contention with the inhabitants of the land:
For there is no faithfulness and there is no steadfast love
and there is no knowledge of God in the land
²*Swearing and lying and murder*
and violent stealing and adultery
and blood upon blood they shed
³*Therefore the land mourns*
and all who dwell in it languish
With the beasts of the field
and with the birds of the skies
yes, even the fish of the sea are taken away
⁴*But let no one contend*
and let none reprove.

And your people are like the contentions of a priest
    5*And you shall stumble by day*
       and the prophet also will stumble with you by night
       and I will destroy your mother
6*My people are destroyed for lack of knowledge*
    because you have rejected knowledge
      so I reject you from being priest to me
 And since you have forgotten the law of your God
    I will forget your children—even I
7*The more they increased the more they sinned against me*
    I will change their glory into dishonor
8*They feed on the sin of my people*
    and have desire toward their iniquity
9*So it shall be like people like priest.*

 I will punish him for his ways
    and requite him for his deeds
10*They shall eat and not be satisfied*
    they insist on playing the harlot but will not multiply
 For they have forsaken Yahweh
    to cherish 11*harlotry and wine.*

 New wine takes away the mind of 12*my people*
    He inquires of his thing of wood
      and his staff gives him oracles
 For a spirit of harlotry has led him astray
    and they have played the harlot out from under their God
13*On the tops of the mountains they sacrifice*
    and on the hills they burn offerings
 Under oak, poplar, and terebinth
    because their shade is good!
 Therefore your daughters play the harlot
    and your sons' brides commit adultery

¹⁴*I will not punish your daughters when they play the harlot*
nor your brides when they commit adultery
For those men over there go aside with harlots
and sacrifice with sacred prostitutes
So a people without understanding will be thrust down.

¹⁵*Though you play the harlot, Israel*
let not Judah become guilty
And do not enter Gilgal
and do not go up to Beth-aven
and do not swear "As Yahweh lives"
¹⁶*Indeed like a stubborn heifer*
Israel is stubborn
Can Yahweh now feed them
like a lamb in a broad pasture?
¹⁷*Ephraim is joined to idols*
Let him alone!
¹⁸*Their drink is gone*
they continually insist to play the harlot
They love, they give
dishonor her shield
¹⁹*A wind has wrapped her in its wings*
and they shall be ashamed of their altars.

THE POETRY HERE IS continuous in the Hebrew Bible, there
being no section marks until the end of v. 19. But two portions appear to be delimited by broken bicolons functioning
as inclusios, 4b–9a and 11b–14, suggesting for the whole
five brief prophetic utterances combined into one: (1) vv.
1–4a, (2) vv. 4b–9a, (3) vv. 9b–11a, (4) vv. 11b–14, and (5)
vv. 15–19. Here are present some of Hosea's major themes:
violation of law and covenant; no steadfast love (*ḥesed*);
no knowledge of God; wicked priests and false prophets;

widespread harlotry, adultery, and drunkenness; and pagan worship on hills and in the sanctuaries. Receiving special emphasis is guilt being attributed to everyone, for which reason no one can contend (v. 4a).

YAHWEH'S CONTENTION WITH INHABITANTS OF THE LAND (HOS 4:1–4A)

Hosea begins as he did in 2:2, saying that Yahweh has a legal case against all inhabitants of the land. He is the plaintiff making the indictment, and will also be the judge (12:2). The indictment contains three key words, all of which relate to the covenant: no faithfulness, no steadfast love, no knowledge of God. This is further spelled out by specifying what has been going on (4:2): false swearing of oaths (10:4), lying, murder, violent stealing (7:1), and adultery (cf. Job 24:15–16). Blood and more blood is being shed (cf. Mic 7:2; Isa 1:15). Jeremiah later lists a string of covenant wrongdoings in one of his temple oracles (Jer 7:9). Because of all this the land mourns and people of the land languish (4:3). A severe drought has come. Beasts of the field and birds overhead are affected (cf. Jer 12:4; 14:2–6), also fish in the sea. The entire creation suffers because of Israel's violation of its covenant with Yahweh (Isa 24:3–6; Joel 1:18). Because of this no one is in a position to contend with Yahweh in the case he is bringing. The concluding word in v. 4a serves also to introduce what follows.

YOUR PEOPLE ARE LIKE THE CONTENTIONS OF A PRIEST (HOS 4:4B–9A)

The first line of poetry is difficult, but the Hebrew appears to censure both people and priests. The KJV reads the line: "For thy people are as they that strive with the priests."

However, the RSV and NRSV emend the text to read: "for with you is my contention, O priest," which has Yahweh focusing blame entirely on the priest. This cannot be correct, as the people are also being censured. If the colon carries forward what precedes, Yahweh's controversy is with everyone. Also, this colon of poetry is discontinuous with a parallel colon in v. 9a, making an inclusio for the poem. And the last colon, which is perfectly clear, metes out judgment to both people and priest. It reads: "So it shall be like people like priest."

Returning to the first colon, I would translate: "And your people are like the contentions of a priest," where an elliptical expression means: "And your people (and their contentions) are like the contentions of a priest." Priests teach the law and judge (Deut 17:8–13; 21:5; 33:10; Jer 18:18), but they can bring the privilege of their office into disrepute by unwarranted contending, like what happened in Korah's rebellion in the wilderness (Num 16). Unwarranted contending is assumed here. The Babylonian Talmud (*Shab.* 149b; *Kid.* 70b) renders the phrase, "your people are like quarrelsome priests." But Yahweh is not focusing on quarrelsome priests, rather on people who are unnecessarily quarrelsome. But whose people? Most likely the king's, which would be all people. Hosea addresses the king in 5:1; speaks disparagingly of the king, princes, and people in 7:3–7, 8:4, and 13:10; and announces judgment on the king, the people, or both, in 3:4; 8:10; and 10:7, 14–15. Even the people have become disenchanted with kings (10:3), which is no surprise given the succession of bad kings in Israel's final days. Yahweh here is addressing the king and saying that the contentions of his people are like unwarranted contentions of a priest.

We move on to judgment. The king will stumble by day, and with him the prophet by night (4:5). Prophets giving the king oracles are called fools in 9:7. Micah says prophets are divining for money (Mic 3:11). The king's mother will also be destroyed (cf. Jer 13:18; 22:26). Yahweh goes on to say that his people are destroyed for lack of knowledge (4:6a). The audience then shifts abruptly, with a focus now on the priest. Yahweh's people are destroyed because the priest has rejected knowledge (cf. 4:1), so Yahweh is going to reject the priest (4:6b). The priest has also forgotten God's law (8:1), a very serious charge, so Yahweh will forget his children (9:11-14, 16-17). The more people increased the more they sinned, so Yahweh will change their glory into dishonor (4:7). The Masora corrects the Hebrew to "they changed" (*tiqqun soferim*) to avoid assigning changeability to God and so offending God (cf. Jer 2:11; Ps 106:20); but the Hebrew text can stand (so the RSV).

Priests are feeding on the sins of people (4:8); that is, they are getting rich on them. Reference could be to sin offerings (cf. Lev 10:17), with the greedy behavior of Eli's sons looming in the background (1 Sam 2:12-17, 29). Micah says priests are teaching for hire (Mic 3:11). The concluding colon of this prophetic word sums up the sad state of affairs: people will suffer the same fate as their priests. Everyone will be judged because everyone is guilty and no one has the right to contend—with anyone else or with Yahweh (4:4a). The legal process is rendered inoperative when those judging are themselves guilty. Hosea mounts similar arguments in 4:11-14 and 8:9-13.

PUNISHMENT FOR EVIL WAYS AND DEEDS (HOS 4:9B-11A)

The straightforward words of vv. 9b-11a make explicit the message of vv. 4b-9a. Yahweh says he will punish either the priest or the king for his ways and doings. People will eat but not be satisfied (cf. Mic 6:14); they will play the harlot but not multiply. The desired effect of sexual rituals is to bring about fertility, but this will not happen. The prophet is now the speaking voice: All have forsaken Yahweh for the lure of harlotry and wine (cf. Isa 28:7).

NEW WINE TAKES AWAY THE MIND OF MY PEOPLE (HOS 4:11B–14)

This poetry contains another broken bicolon forming an inclusio for the speech. Yahweh resumes speaking in the first person, and his message is the same as before: Everyone is guilty of wrongdoing. The speech begins by picking up on the wine last mentioned, with Yahweh saying now that new wine takes away the mind of his people (4:11). The diviner is inquiring of his thing of wood and asking his staff for oracles (v. 12; Hab 2:19; Jer 2:27; 10:8; cf. Deut 18:10). Other prophets condemn such individuals (Mic 3:7; Jer 27:9; 29:8). The "thing of wood" (Hos 4:12) could be the Asherah (Judg 16:25; Deut 16:21), a tree or wooden pillar representing the Canaanite mother goddess, or possibly a diviner's oak (cf. Judg 9:37). Either would be evidence of a spirit of harlotry that has led people astray. Hosea refers to this "spirit of harlotry" again in 5:4, where he says that because of it people do not know Yahweh. Sacrifices and burnt offerings fill the mountains and hills with smoke, and daughters and young brides are carrying on harlotry and adultery under oak, poplar, and terebinth, benefiting from the shade they provide (Hos 4:13; Deut 12:2; Jer 2:20; 3:6; 1 Kgs 14:23; 2 Kgs 17:10). There is irony in these words! Then in Hos 4:14 Yahweh turns from indictment to judgment. Yahweh is both accuser and judge. He will not judge the daughters and young brides, because men standing nearby are doing much the same thing—sacrificing with sacred prostitutes (v. 14; cf. Deut 23:17–18). The speech closes by saying that a people without understanding will be brought down.

STAY OUT OF THE SANCTUARIES! (HOS 4:15–19)

In this final segment of poetry Judah is cautioned not to play the harlot as Israel has. This is not necessarily a gloss, as some take it, since there are fifteen references to Judah in the book (1:1, 7, 11; 4:15; 5:5, 10, 12, 13, 14; 6:4, 11; 8:14; 10:11; 11:12; 12:2), and Hosea is reported to have been active during the reigns of Uzziah, Jotham, Ahaz, and Hezekiah in Judah (1:1). Judgment of Judah would be understandable during the reign of Ahaz (compare Isaiah), also hope during the early reign of Hezekiah when there was reform. The prophet here seems to be the speaker. Hosea says not to enter Israel's sanctuaries at Gilgal and Bethel (4:15), where Gilgal is doubtless the well-known sanctuary near Jericho (Josh 4:19–24; Hos 9:15; 12:11; Amos 4:4; 5:5), and "Beth-aven" ("House of Wickedness") a place near the city of Bethel (Gen 28:19; Josh 7:2; 1 Sam 13:5), or more likely the Bethel sanctuary itself where Jeroboam erected his idolatrous calf (1 Kgs 12:28–30; Hos 8:4–6; 13:2; Amos 3:14; 4:4; 5:5). Yet God spoke to Jacob at Bethel (Hos 12:4; cf. Gen 28:18–22). Hosea is familiar with the Jacob tradition, referring to Jacob's grasping brother Esau's heel in the womb, his sojourning at Bethel on his way to Laban's house in Syria where he herded sheep for two wives, his struggle at the Jabbok with a divine messenger on the way to meet Esau, and finally the emotional reunion with his estranged brother (Hos 12:3–4, 12). People are no longer to swear oaths in Yahweh's name, because they are either ingenuine or directed to idols of other gods (cf. Jer 4:1–2).

The nation is then characterized as a stubborn heifer (Hos 4:16; cf. Deut 32:15), and can Yahweh feed such an intractable beast? No. Ephraim is joined to idols (4:17), perhaps a reference to the calves at Dan and Bethel, and perhaps to another at Samaria (8:4–6; 13:2). Hosea calls North Israel Ephraim, after the preeminent tribe of the north (Isa 7:9). The prophet says to leave him alone. More irony (*epitrope*). People insist on playing the harlot. Amos and Isaiah have strong words from Yahweh about Israel's festivals and solemn assemblies (Amos 5:21; Isa 1:13–14), and Hosea talks about an end to them (Hos 9:1–9). The next line is difficult. People love and give (themselves?) to what they are doing; dishonor is their shield (4:18). But things will end with a wind coming to wrap Israel in its wings, alluding to exile (4:19; 13:15; cf. Isa 57:13), and one day they will be ashamed of their altars (8:11).

REFLECTION

1. Are we as concerned with covenant violation today as Hosea was? What can we do about swearing, lying, murder, stealing, adultery, and other wrongdoings? And what about faithfulness, steadfast love, and knowledge of God?

2. Is there not a correlation between Hosea's message about Yahweh's own willingness to suspend judgment of interaction with other gods and cultic prostitutes and Jesus's words about taking a log out of another's eye when a log is in one's own (Matt 7:1–5)?

3. Can people be destroyed for a lack of knowledge? And what about forgetting the law of God and the commandments of Jesus?

4. What are idols of worship in the present day? Are any of these idols worshiped in our houses of worship? If so, what can we do about that?

10

"YOUR STEADFAST LOVE IS LIKE MORNING MIST" (HOS 6:4-11A)

6 4*What shall I do with you, Ephraim?*
what shall I do with you, Judah?
Your steadfast love is like morning mist
like the dew going early away
5*Therefore I have hewn by the prophets*
I have slain with words of my mouth
and your judgment goes forth as light
6*For I delight in steadfast love and not sacrifice*
and knowledge of God rather than burnt offerings
7*But they like others transgressed the covenant*
there they dealt faithlessly with me
8*Gilead is a city of evildoers*
foot-tracked in blood
9*And as marauding bands lie in wait for a man*
priests band together

They murder on the road to Shechem
   indeed they commit wickedness
¹⁰In the house of Israel I have seen a horrible thing
   Ephraim's harlotry is there
     Israel is defiled
¹¹Also Judah, for you a harvest is appointed.

WHAT SHALL I DO WITH YOU, O EPHRAIM?
(HOS 6:4–11A)

THESE VERSES, THOUGH NOT delimited by section markers, appear nevertheless to be a unit in the Hebrew Bible with v. 11b belonging to chapter 12. A section marking comes at the end of v 11. Yahweh is the speaker, opening the oracle by asking in exasperation what he is to do with Israel and Judah. Here again Hosea probes the inner disposition of a God who is struggling (11:8–9). The oracle is about "steadfast love" (*ḥesed*), an important word for Hosea, referring to covenant love that must be kept. The term appears also with great frequency in the Psalms. Yahweh shows steadfast love to those who keep his commandments (Exod 20:6; 34:6–7; Deut 5:10; 7:9), but Hosea says people do not show it in return (Hos 4:1). Yahweh's faithfulness, steadfast love, and mercies never cease; they are new every morning (Lam 3:22–23).

Yahweh says Israel's steadfast love is like morning mist, like dew going early away. The KJV, RSV, and NRSV translate the Hebrew as "cloud," but this makes sense only if we imagine a cloud of mist or fog. The JB rendering is "mist," which is better. The same two terms appear in 13:3 where Hosea says people kissing calves "will be like morning fog / mist, and like the dew going early away."

People have been hewn by the prophets, whom Hosea calls elsewhere the watchmen of Ephraim (9:8; Jer 6:17;

Ezek 3:17). There is power in the prophetic word (Jer 5:14). Yahweh can fell people with a single word (Luther). Yahweh delights in steadfast love (Mic 7:18) more than sacrifice, in knowledge of God more than burnt offerings (Hos 6:6). Hebrew *ʾadam* should be taken here as men in general (cf. Ps 82:7 KJV; Job 31:33 RSV) or as humankind, or it could be rendered simply as "others," which is how the NRSV translates in Job 31:33. The RSV and NRSV follow the Targum and Vulgate by translating the colon: "But at Adam they transgressed the covenant." However, Genesis says nothing about any covenant made with Adam. A broken covenant is referred to in Hos 8:1, and covenants made with empty oaths in 10:4. The eighth-century prophets, including Isaiah, say very little about covenant.

"There," in North Israel, they dealt faithlessly with Yahweh (Hos 6:7, 10). Gilead is referred to here as a city, which must be some unspecified location in the territory of Gilead in the central Transjordan highlands between the Yarmuk River and Heshbon. Ramoth-Gilead (1Kings 22; 2 Kgs 8:28—9:14) is a specific location, today a border crossing between Syria and Jordan. There Israel got involved in worship of other gods during the period of the Judges (Judges 10), but more violent activity could have been going on there recently (12:11). The charge of Gilead being "foot-tracked with blood" (6:8) makes a play on the name Jacob (= Israel), which Hosea does again in 12:3. In 734 BC Tiglath-pileser and the Assyrians destroyed the entire Transjordan, including Gilead.

Priests again come in for censure for banding together like bands of marauders, waiting to attack the unaware (6:9). They are murdering people on the way to Shechem, a road evidently notorious for highway robberies (Judg 9:25), like the Jericho road cited in the New Testament (Luke 10:30). Yahweh says he has seen a "horrible thing" in the house of

Israel (6:10; cf. Jer 18:13), for harlotry abounds there. In conclusion Yahweh adds that an unwelcome harvest awaits Judah (6:11; cf. Jer 51:33), which returns to the beginning of the oracle where Yahweh is wondering what he can do with Israel and Judah. "Harvest" refers to an upcoming exile.

REFLECTION

1. Is there a danger of steadfast love fading or disappearing in the walk of faith, and if so, what can be done about it?

2. Does the prophetic word cut deeply into people today, and who is speaking it? Does your pastor or priest speak prophetic words, and if so, what are they?

3. Does steadfast adherence to the covenant count for more than offerings in today's worship?

4. What today would be considered harlotry, defiling the nation or the people of God?

11

"WHEN ISRAEL WAS A BOY I LOVED HIM" (HOS 11:1-11)

11 ¹ *When Israel was a boy I loved him*
        and out of Egypt I called my son
    ² *They called them*
        thus they went from me
    To the Baals they sacrificed
        and to idols they burned incense
    ³ *Yet I, I taught Ephraim to walk*
        taking them by his arms
            and they did not know that I healed them
    ⁴ *With ropes of men I led them*
        with cords of love
    And I was to them
        as one lifting up a yoke upon their jaws
            and I bent down to him, I gave to eat

5 *Will he not return to the land of Egypt*
    and Assyria, will it be his king?
        for they refuse to return
6 *The sword will whirl about in his cities*
    and consume its bars
        yes it will devour their plans
7 *My people is hung up on turning from me*
    so to the yoke they are called
        and together they will not lift it
8 *How can I give you up, O Ephraim!*
    can I deliver you up, O Israel!
  How can I make you like Admah!
    and treat you like Zeboiim!
  My heart turns against me
    altogether my compassion grows warm and tender
9 *I will not execute my burning anger*
    I will not again destroy Ephraim
        for I am God and not man
  The Holy One in your midst
    and I will not come into the city
10 *They shall go after Yahweh*
    he will roar like a lion
  Indeed he will roar
    and his sons will come trembling from the sea
11 *They will come trembling as a bird from Egypt*
    and as a dove from the land of Assyria
  And I will return them to their houses
            oracle of Yahweh.

HOW CAN I GIVE YOU UP, O EPHRAIM! (HOSEA 11:1–11)

YAHWEH SPEAKS DIRECTLY TO Israel in this self-contained oracle, concluding as it does with an oracle formula at the end of v. 11. Yahweh begins using a father-son image to describe the covenant relation, saying that when Israel was a boy he loved him. Isaiah also used the image of a caring parent to describe Yahweh's early rearing of Israel (Isa 1:2). Love is the controlling divine attribute in the present oracle, despite Israel's rebellion and a need for Yahweh to punish. Yahweh called his son out of Egypt, out of a house of slavery (Exod 4:22), which Matthew in the New Testament recasts to describe the "calling" of baby Jesus from Egypt after Mary and Joseph's sojourn there (Matt 2:15). In the case of Israel, however, the Baals too made their call, and people responded by going far from Yahweh. They sacrificed to the Baals and burned incense to their idols.

Yahweh reflects more on his early parental love. He taught Ephraim (= Israel) to walk. The text is difficult, but Yahweh seems to be saying that he took the young child by the arms when he was making his first steps (11:3; cf. 7:15). Another reading is that Yahweh took the young child up into his arms (RSV, NRSV; cf. Deut 1:31; Isa 63:9). Either image will suffice. The lad also had childhood sicknesses and knew not that Yahweh healed them (11:3; cf. 5:13; 7:1). Doctors there were in Egypt and elsewhere (Gen 50:2; Jer 8:22), but the healer in Israel was Yahweh (Exod 15:26). Israel appears to have known this (6:1).

The image shifts in 11:4 to a kind owner and his working animal. The expression "ropes of men" is strange, but taken with "cords of love" and with what follows they make several references to Yahweh's gentle leading of his people. Finally, Yahweh is like one who lifts up the yoke on the jaw of a working animal so it can eat more easily (cf. 10:11).

Then comes an indictment because of Israel's ingratitude for all this kindness (13:6). The Hebrew term usually rendered a negative may here be an asseverative, in which case the meaning is that Israel will *surely* return to Egypt (cf. 7:16; 8:13; 9:3, 6; 11:5) and also to Assyria, who will rule them (9:3; 10:6; 11:5). Hosea sees no use in people calling on Egypt and Assyria for help (5:13; 7:11; 8:9; 12:1; 14:3). Exile is on the horizon. These two undesired destinations for a stubborn and ungrateful people are supported by the prophet's words in 9:3, 6. Israel will go to both places because it refuses to return to Yahweh (11:5; cf. Jer 8:5). Israel is a stubborn and rebellious son, in Hos 4:16 a stubborn heifer. Judgment continues. Swords will whirl about in Israel's cities (11:6); bars of city gates and houses will be consumed by fire (8:14; cf. Jer 51:30). The swords here are almost personified (cf. Jer 47:6–7; Ezek 14:17), denoting war in all its terrible facets (Jer 50:35–37). Actions carried out by the enemy will end all plans by Israel's defenders. Yahweh repeats in a difficult expression the people's insistence on turning from him, and because of this another yoke will be put upon them that cannot be lifted even with outside help (11:7). How different from when Israel bore Yahweh's yoke (Hos 11:4)! With Yahweh the yoke was easy (said also of Jesus's yoke in Matt 11:29–30), but with an enemy it will not be.

Yahweh then gives another insight into his inner disposition, something occurring nowhere else in the entire Old Testament, with the single exception of Jer 31:20. Amos never speaks like this about Yahweh, nor Micah. The oracle now turns to divine speech in the first person. Yahweh says he can hardly bear to think of giving Ephraim up, of turning Israel over to another (11:8). How could he make his people like Admah and Zeboiim, cities overthrown with Sodom and Gomorrah (Deut 29:23)?

The humanizing of Yahweh's inner nature continues. Yahweh's heart recoils within him; his inner feelings grow warm and tender (11:8; cf. Gen 43:30; 1 Kgs 3:26). Nothing like this is heard in any other prophet. Yahweh thinks he cannot execute his burning anger and destroy Ephraim, for he is God and not man (11:9). Yet his anger burns at the sight of Samaria's idolatrous calves (8:5; 10:5; 13:2). Yahweh, perhaps because he is the Holy One in Israel's midst, will not enter the city, presumably Samaria. Some emend the Hebrew to say that Yahweh will *not* come to destroy (so RSV, NRSV), which yields no sense here or anywhere else in the book. Yes, Yahweh has struggled mightily over having to exercise judgment, but make no mistake about it: judgment will come.

The oracle then turns abruptly to a time after Israel's cities are destroyed, when people will hear Yahweh roaring like a lion (11:10; cf. 5:14; 13:7) and go trembling after him—from the sea (or the west), the south, and the north, and then Yahweh will return them to their houses (11:11). People in Northern Israel have fled south at the approach of the Assyrians. The refugees not only swell Jerusalem's size, but some go on to settle in Egypt. Others apparently go west to the Mediterranean coast and perhaps even farther to the Greek islands. Those coming from Assyria are exiles taken there by the Assyrians after Samaria and all Northern Israel are destroyed.

REFLECTION

1. Israel and the church has always affirmed that God called it into being. Do you have a sense of being called, or is that something applying only to pastors, priests, and missionaries?

2. Are there other voices out there calling people? What are they?

3. Can we talk today about the Lord helping us to grow during childhood and adolescence, and of bringing

healing when we are sick—or is all of this left to doctors and the wonders of modern science?

4. How do you feel about Hosea's insights into the inner disposition of God? Is it meaningful to speak of God as being torn in heart and warm and tender in compassion?

12

"RETURN, ISRAEL, TO YAHWEH YOUR GOD" (HOS 14:1-7)

14 ¹*Return Israel*
   to Yahweh your God
     for you have stumbled in your iniquity
  ²*Take with you words*
   and return to Yahweh
    say to him:
  "Take away all iniquity
   and accept good
    and we offer calves on our lips
  ³*Assyria will not save us*
   on a horse we will not ride
  And we will no more say 'our god'
   to the work of our hands
    you by whom the orphan finds mercy.

4*I will heal their turning away*
  I will love them freely
    for my anger has turned from him
5*I will be as dew to Israel*
  he shall blossom as a lily
    and he shall strike out his roots as Lebanon
6*His shoots shall spread out*
  and his splendor be as the olive
    and his fragrance as Lebanon
7*They shall return and dwell in its shadow*
  they shall grow grain
  They shall send out shoots as the vine
    its remembrance as the wine of Lebanon.

RETURN WITH THESE WORDS
(HOS 14:1–7)

THESE VERSES ARE DELIMITED by section markings in
the Hebrew Bible, forming a fitting conclusion to Hosea's
prophecies of indictment and judgment, struggles within
the divine mind over having to cast off his beloved people,
also indications of hope once judgment has taken place.
A passage similar to the present one occurs in 5:15—6:3,
but some think that confession is ingenuine because of the
indictment following. It may not be. The last verses of the
chapter and also the book are add-ons—v. 8 asking rhetorically what Yahweh has to do with idols, and v. 9 a word to
the wise urging such a one to understand that the ways of
Yahweh are right, with upright people walking in them
and transgressors stumbling (5:5; 14:1). The word from the
prophet here is a call for Israel to return (v. 1), followed by
words it can use in response to Yahweh should it decide
to return (vv. 2–3), and then Yahweh's promise of healing

and acceptance (vv. 4–7). Hosea's prophecies thus end on a strong note of hope.

"Return" is the keyword, which in Hebrew can also be translated "repent." If Israel is to return, it must return to Yahweh its God. People have stumbled in their iniquity; they have met with calamity. The words find a later echo in Jeremiah (Jer 3:22; 4:1; 6:21; 18:15). People are to ask Yahweh to take away all iniquity and accept what is good. The final colon of v. 2 contains an unusual expression. People are to offer "calves" on their lips, which is strange, but since idolatrous calves at Israel's sanctuaries have contributed not a little to Israel's iniquity, this may be an enigmatic reversal the sense of which is now lost to us. People in any case are now promising proper offerings to Yahweh. Many follow the Greek LXX and read "fruit of our lips" (cf. Isa 57:18; Prov 12:14; 18:20), which makes more sense. Nevertheless, the Hebrew remains obscure.

What is clear is that people have come to realize that Assyria cannot save them, reversing an earlier hope that it could (5:13; 7:11; 8:9; 12:1), and any idea of riding horses to meet this foe is abandoned (10:13; cf. Isa 30:16; Ps 33:16–17). Reference to horses may also point to a reliance upon Egypt (cf. Isa 31:1), which would also prove futile (7:11). Besides Yahweh there is no savior (13:4). More importantly, people will no more address idols as "our god" (4:17; 8:4, 6; 11:2; 13:2; Isa 42:17), where the expression "work of our hands" commonly refers to idols (Mic 5:13; Isa 2:8; 37:19; Jer 25:6–7). Israel is left an orphan after suffering defeat (cf. Lam 5:3), but knows that with Yahweh the orphan finds mercy (cf. John 14:18).

A chastened and penitent people is answered. Yahweh says he will heal their turning away and love them freely. Yahweh's anger has turned away; it does not last forever (Mic 7:18; Ps 103:9). Yahweh will now be refreshing and regenerating dew, reversing an earlier complaint that Israel's steadfast love was like dew going early away (6:4; 13:3). References to lily blossoms and scented, sturdy cedars of Lebanon are reminiscent of the Song of Songs (Song 2:1–2, 13; 3:9; 4:11; 5:13, 15; 6:11). The olive tree is also beautiful (Jer 11:16). Hosea mixes metaphors with literal promises of future beauty and plenty. Israel will grow and once again be beautiful. It shall return to Yahweh, which is most important, and dwell in shady places, the mark of peace and contentment (1 Kgs 4:25; Mic 4:4; Zech 3:10). People will again grow and harvest grain, which earlier was denied (7:14; 8:7; 9:2), and vineyards will produce grapes for wine, another reversal of Yahweh's prior judgment (2:9, 12; 7:14; 9:2). This wine will be like the fine wine of Lebanon.

REFLECTION

1. Do you find repentance hard? Why, and where can you find help?

2. Does it help if God supplies you with words of confession? What about confessions recited in worship? Does this have anything to do with what Paul says in Rom 8:26?

3. Is it sometimes necessary to reverse earlier denials with later affirmations? Recall Jesus's words to Peter in John 21:15–17.

4. When you read Yahweh's response to this confession, do you sense the deep love he has for his people, particularly in light of Hosea's words and images drawn from the Song of Songs?

MICAH

13

"WOE FOR THOSE WHO DEVISE WICKEDNESS" (MIC 2:1-11)

2 ¹Woe for those who devise wickedness
   and evil deeds on their beds!
   Then in the light of morning they do it
   because it is within their power
   ²They covet fields and they seize
   and houses, and they take
   And they oppress a fellow and his house
   a man and his ancestral inheritance.

³Therefore thus said Yahweh:
   Look, I am devising evil against this family
   from which you cannot remove your necks
   And you shall not walk haughtily
   for it will be an evil time
⁴On that day a taunt song will be uttered over you
   and a wailing lament wailed, declaring:

"We are utterly ruined
   he changes the portion of my people
How he takes it away from me
   to the apostate he apportions our fields"
5 Therefore there will not be for you
   anyone to cast out the line by lot
      in the assembly of Yahweh

6 "Talk not," they talk
   "they should not talk of these things"
   "Reproaches will surely cease"
      7 the house of Jacob says
   Is Yahweh's spirit impatient?
      are these his doings?
   Do not my words do good
      with one who walks uprightly?
8 But recently my people
   for the enemy you raised up
From the front of a garment
   you strip off a cloak
From trusting passersby
   as though they were prisoners of war
9 The women of my people you drive out
   from their lovely houses
From her children you take away
   my glory forever
10 "Get up and go
   for this is no place to rest"
   On account of uncleanness that destroys
      yes, a sickening destruction
11 If a man were to go about
   uttering hot air and lies:
   "I will talk to you about wine and beer"
      he would be the talker for this people!

WOE TO THOSE WHO DEVISE WICKEDNESS (MICAH 2:1–2)

THE PRESENT VERSES CONSIST of a threat to those who think up evil and do it (vv. 1–2), Yahweh's judgment in like measure against them (vv. 3–5), and a word from Micah to those who don't want to hear judgment talk (vv. 6–11). The text in places is difficult, particularly in vv. 6–11, but the general sense is clear. The first two passages focus on the wealthy, who are in violation of the tenth commandment (Exod 20:17; Deut 5:21).

Micah begins by declaring woe on those who think up evil at night while lying on their beds. "Woe" is an invective coming close to a curse, heard also from Amos (Amos 5:18; 6:1), Hosea (Hos 7:13; 9:12), Isaiah (Isa 1:4; 5:8–25), and other prophets (Nah 3:1; Hab 2:6–19; Zeph 2:5; 3:1; Jer 22:13; 23:1; Ezek 13:3, 18). In Matthew's Gospel blessings conferred on followers of Jesus are contrasted with woes pronounced on the scribes and Pharisees (Matt 5:3–11; 23:13–36). Micah says those who lie awake at night devising evil (2:1; cf. Ps 36:4) carry out their plans in the morning, for it is within their power to do it (cf. Gen 31:29). Who are these people, and what are they doing? They are wealthy landowners coveting fields and houses of the poor, then going on to seize them (Mic 2:2 Isa 5:8; Amos 4:1). Holdings of the wealthy increased during the long and prosperous reign of Uzziah (r. 783–742 BC). Coveting another's property, forbidden in the tenth commandment, included aggressive practices depriving fellow Israelites of their ancestral inheritance. Kings were doing it. We know what happened to Naboth the Jezreelite, whose ancestral inheritance was seized by King Ahab, and how judgment came to him from the prophet Elijah (1 Kgs 21). Isaiah, Micah's contemporary, declared woe on those "who join house to house, who add field to field" (Isa 5:8). Some losing their fields and houses were probably unable to pay debts, bringing hardship on entire households, resulting even in family members—including children—being forced into slavery. Widows were particularly vulnerable (2 Kgs 4:1–7).

Deuteronomy shows a particular concern for those having no inheritance (landed property), viz., sojourners, orphans, widows, and resident Levites, who in the seventh century BC were out of a job. Deuteronomy contained laws protecting widows, Levites, and the poor (Deut 14:27; 24:6–7, 10–15, 17). A third-year charity tithe was established for the poor and needy (Deut 14:28–29), and a law of debt remission was enacted so no poor would exist among the people, which was followed up by an admonition that one not harden one's heart in lending to the poor (Deut 15:1–11). Deuteronomy required manumitting Hebrew slaves after six years (Deut 15:12–18; cf. Exod 21:2–11) and provided no-interest loans to fellow Israelites (Deut 23:19–20). At harvest time the sojourner, orphan, and widow were accorded gleaning rights (Deut 24:19–22). Even more important, Deuteronomy taught that justice must not be perverted toward the sojourner, orphan, and widow (Deut 24:17; 27:19). Yahweh loves them and treats them justly (Deut 10:17–18), so Israelites must do likewise. Israelites were to remember that they were once a band of slaves in Egypt (Deut 10:19; 16:12; 24:18, 22). Isaiah said justice was "rescuing the oppressed, defending the orphan, and pleading for the widow" (Isa 1:17), and it was not being done (Isa 1:23; 10:2).

YAHWEH IS DEVISING EVIL AGAINST THIS FAMILY (MIC 2:3–5)

Well, Yahweh has a counterplan (Mic 2:3). Yahweh too had been thinking about what to do with a family of greedy landowners, where "family" might better be translated "gang" (cf. Jer 8:3). A yoke will be placed upon these individuals, and they will not be able to remove it from their necks (cf. Jer 28:14). People will be enslaved, perhaps by Assyrians entering their land. Yahweh says that with a yoke on their neck people will not be able to walk upright as the haughty do, a theme given expanded treatment by Isaiah (Isa 2:9–17; 3:16–23; 5:15), for it will be an evil time.

Yahweh tells these people on that unwelcomed day a taunt song will be heard over you, but the wailing will be your wailing—wailing of the dispossessed rich. Yes, you will be utterly ruined because Yahweh is changing land portions of his people, taking away ill-gotten houses and fields and giving them to an enemy. Yahweh says that what you have done to others—grabbing land, fields, and houses—will now be done to you (Mic 2:4). Punishment will befit crime. Then you might just as well forget about casting out boundary lines by lot in Yahweh's assembly (Mic 2:5; cf. Josh 13–21).

DO NOT TALK OF SUCH THINGS! (MIC 2:6–11)

This final word appears to be from Micah to those not wanting to hear his preaching. People are telling him and probably others that they should not talk about such things. Other prophets were given similar pushbacks (Isa 30:10 Amos 2:12; 5:10; 7:12–13, 16; Jer 5:12; 11:21). Reproaches of this kind will surely end. People ask, "Is Yahweh becoming impatient? Are these his doings?" (Mic 2:7).

Then the prophet answers his critics. He asks if his words are not doing good to those who walk uprightly (2:7). The Hebrew here is difficult. Micah seems to be saying that Yahweh has raised up an enemy against his people and they are acting violently, stripping off outer garments from innocent passersby as if they were prisoners of war (2:8). Yahweh is doing the very thing the rich landlords were doing! Yahweh is driving women out of nice homes (2:9a; Isa 5:9), as creditors were doing to women not paying their debts. And her children, who were Yahweh's pride and glory, are being taken away (2:9b). Women are being told to get up and leave their houses; they will no longer be places for them to rest. On account of this unclean wrongdoing has come a sickening destruction (2:10). Micah ends his rebuke by returning to the beginning, saying that if someone came along uttering hot air and lies, talking to people about wine and beer (2:11; Isa 5:11, 22), he would be the talker for this people!

REFLECTION

1. Do you see in this prophecy a rebuke of those who violate the tenth commandment? Is coveting simply an interior disposition, or does it conceal a real desire to steal what belongs to another, which would be a violation of the eighth commandment?

2. Do we have laws today protecting the vulnerable in our society from wealthy landowners and creditors who are greedy for more land, fields, and houses? And what are we to say about lawyers who defend such landowners and creditors?

3. Do you believe that God metes out punishment corresponding to one's sinful acts, or does the love of God

as revealed in the New Testament bring something else? What are we to make of Paul's words in Rom 2:4–11?

4. Do we like to hear preaching from someone like Micah, or do we prefer preachers who speak empty, deceptive words catering to base human desires?

14

"ZION SHALL BE PLOWED AS A FIELD" (MIC 3:1–12)

3 ¹*And I said:*
  Hear now, heads of Jacob
    and rulers of the house of Israel!
      Is it not for you to know justice?
  ²*Haters of good and lovers of evil*
    tearers of skin from them
      and their flesh from off their bones
  ³*And who eat the flesh of my people*
    and strip the skin off them
      and their bones they break in pieces
  And they spread them out as in a pot
    and as flesh in a caldron
  ⁴*Then they cry out to Yahweh*
    but he will not answer them
  Yes, he will hide his face from them at that time
    because they have done evil deeds.

5 *Thus said Yahweh concerning the prophets*
  who mislead my people
 The ones biting with their teeth
  then they cry "Peace"
 But one who does not put something in their mouth
  they declare holy war against him:
6 *Therefore it will be night for you without vision*
  and darkness for you without divination
 The sun will go down on the prophets
  and the day be black on them
7 *And the seers will be embarrassed*
  and the diviners be ashamed
 All of them will cover their lips
  for there is no answer from God
8 *But I, I am filled with power*
  with the spirit of Yahweh
   and justice and might
 To declare to Jacob his transgression
  and to Israel his sin.

9 *Hear now this,*
  heads of the house of Jacob
   and rulers of the house of Israel!
 Who abhor justice
  and pervert all that is right
10 *Who build Zion with bloodshed*
  and Jerusalem with violent injustice!
11 *Its heads give judgment for a bribe*
  and its priests teach for a price
 Its prophets divine for silver
  yet upon Yahweh they lean, saying
 "Is not Yahweh in our midst
  no evil will come upon us"

¹²*Therefore on account of you*
　　Zion shall be plowed as a field
　And Jerusalem shall be a heap of ruins
　　and the mountain of the house high places of a forest.

THE PRESENT VERSES IN the Hebrew Bible are delimited by section markers into three units: (1) vv. 1–4, (2) vv. 5–8, and (3) vv. 9–12. The final passage concludes with a prophecy for which Micah was remembered: "Zion shall be plowed as a field." It was cited at Jeremiah's trial for having preached judgment on Jerusalem and the temple, and aided in his acquittal because elders present pointed out that it went unfulfilled because King Hezekiah humbled himself, feared Yahweh, and entreated Yahweh's favor (Jer 26:17–19).

IS IT NOT FOR YOU TO KNOW JUSTICE?
(MIC 3:1–4)

In the first passage Micah addresses rulers of the nation, asking rhetorically if it is not their responsibility to know justice. These are judges, elders, and probably wealthy landowners. Whether the king is included cannot be ascertained, since Micah, unlike Amos or Hosea, never mentions the king in connection with a perversion of justice. The third passage begins in much the same way as the present one (3:9). Justice here and elsewhere is Micah's major concern. It is also a concern of Isaiah's (Isa 1:17). The nation is addressed as Jacob or Israel, which here refers to the Southern Kingdom of Judah centered in Jerusalem.

The charge is that rulers are haters of good and lovers of evil (3:2). Isaiah complains about those who call evil good and good evil (Isa 5:20). Amos, for his part, says "Hate evil and love good, and establish justice in the gate" (Amos

5:15), but notes that people do hate one who reproves in the gate (Amos 5:10). Ps 97:10 says that one who loves Yahweh hates evil. And Elihu, referring to God, asks rhetorically, "Shall one who hates justice govern?" (Job 34:17). Micah, resorting to a graphic, cannibalistic image, says these lovers of evil are treating weak and helpless victims like one who tears off skin and takes flesh off bones. Worse yet, they are fattening themselves by eating the flesh of Yahweh's people as if they were wild beasts (3:3a). The unsettling imagery continues: victims are boiled in a kettle as if by one cooking up meat for dinner (3:3b).

Those doing these things cry out to Yahweh, but he will not answer them (3:4; cf. Isa 1:15). Jeremiah later says that all evildoers can expect the same (Jer 11:11). But from Second Isaiah we learn that when the bonds of injustice are loosed, when the oppressed go free, when people share their bread with the hungry, when they bring homeless poor into their houses, and when they clothe the naked, their calls to Yahweh will be answered (Isa 58:6–9). But from those engaged in evil deeds Yahweh hides his face (3:4b; cf. Isa 1:15), which means withholding grace or favor.

ON PROPHETS WHO MISLEAD MY PEOPLE (MIC 3:5–8)

The second passage is a divine oracle directed at prophets who mislead people. If given something to eat they cry "peace," but to one not putting something in their mouth they declare holy war (3:5). These are the prophets spoken of in 2:11. The priest at Bethel, not wanting to hear judgment, told Amos to go home and "eat bread there" (Amos 7:12). Amos might then be like other prophets who eat well because of their prophecies! False prophets have their day in the sun (Deut 13:1–5), but a day will dawn when it will be night for them, when darkness will descend without their prophecies (3:6; Jer 28:12–17). The sun will also go down on others who reject Yahweh and fail to turn from their evil ways (Jer 15:9). Indeed, all those practicing divining arts, seers, diviners, and others, will in time be embarrassed and ashamed (3:7; cf. Zech 13:4). Micah says they will cover their lips because no answer is coming from Yahweh. Covering the lips is a sign of shame (Lev 13:45). When prophecies failed, Jeremiah discovered that prophets were nowhere to be found; they disappeared into the woodwork (Jer 37:19). Amos talked about the day when there would be a famine for the word of Yahweh (Amos 8:11–12), a famine of another kind that would affect everyone.

It is unusual to hear Micah speak emphatically about himself being filled with power and Yahweh's spirit, but he knows the true prophet speaks about justice, might, and transgressions (3:8; cf. Isa 58:1). Jeremiah in his day knew prophets who healed wounds lightly crying, "peace, peace, when there was no peace" (Jer 6:14; 8:11).

THOSE WHO ABHOR JUSTICE AND PERVERT WHAT IS RIGHT (MIC 3:9–12)

In the third passage Micah is back to addressing rulers of the nation. They abhor justice and pervert what is right. Zion is filled with bloodshed and violent acts (7:2; Isa 1:15–17). Judges give acquittal for a bribe (7:3; Isa 1:23; 5:23). Deuteronomy has a considerable amount to say about bribes being a perversion of justice (Deut 16:18–20; 27:25; cf. Exod 23:8). Yahweh will not take a bribe (Deut 10:17). Priests teach for the money and prophets do the same (Mic 3:11a). Yet they confidently depend upon Yahweh and believe no evil will come upon them (3:11b; Jer 5:12). Zephaniah leveled a similar indictment of those running the city of Jerusalem (Zeph 3:1–4). But Micah says that on account of these individuals Zion shall be plowed as a field; Jerusalem shall become a heap of ruins, and the "mountain of the house," which is the mount on which Yahweh's temple stands (Isa 2:2–3), shall be reduced to high places with trees growing (Mic 3:12). Isaiah called Jerusalem the "House of the Forest," where building interiors were lined with cedars from Lebanon (Isa 22:8; cf. Jer 22:14–15, 23). Micah uttered a similar judgment on Samaria (1:6).

REFLECTION

1. How concerned are we today that our judges and elected officials know justice and practice justice? Are the poor and helpless treated in shameful ways? If so, what can we do about it?

2. Do you believe that God sometimes hides his face from evildoers when they call, or is he ready to hear anyone 24/7?

3. Do pastors and priests ever minister to people on the basis of being well taken care of financially? How should those holding ministerial office act toward those under their care?

4. Do you believe that your city or your place of worship could be reduced to ruin due to God's judgment, or do these things happen simply by accident or because of natural causes?

15

"BUT YOU, O BETHLEHEM OF EPHRATHAH" (MIC 5:2-9)

5 ²*But you, O Bethlehem of Ephrathah*
  little to be among the clans of Judah
  From you shall come forth for me
    one to be ruler in Israel
  And his origins are of old
    from ancient days
  ³*Therefore he shall deliver them up until the time*
    when she who bears has given birth
  Then a remnant of his kin shall return
    to the children of Israel
  ⁴*And he will stand and rule in the strength of Yahweh*
    in the majesty of the name of Yahweh his God
  And they shall dwell, for now he will be great
    to the ends of the earth
      ⁵*and he will be the One of Peace*

Assyria will indeed come into our land
   and he will indeed tread in our palaces
And we will raise against him seven shepherds
   and eight princes of men
6And they shall rule the land of Assyria with the sword
   and the land of Nimrod in its entrances
And he will deliver from Assyria
   when he comes into our land
     and when he treads within our border.

7And the remnant of Jacob shall be
   in the midst of many peoples
Like dew from Yahweh
   like showers upon grass
Which does not wait for any man
   and does not stay for the sons of men
8And the remnant of Jacob shall be among the nations
   in the midst of many peoples
Like a lion among the beasts of the forest
   like a young lion among the flocks of sheep
Which if it goes through and tramples
   and tears in pieces, then none can deliver
9Your hand shall be lifted up over your adversaries
   and all your enemies shall be cut off.

HERE IN THE MIDDLE of the book of Micah, after devastating preaching in chapters 1–3 and before more of the same in chapter 6 and the beginning of 7, come words of hope from the prophet. In the present verses are two hope prophecies, 5:2–6 and 5:7–9, which are delimited by sections in the Hebrew Bible. In the first Yahweh promises to raise up a king like David to deliver Israel from Assyria; in the second a remnant of Israel will become triumphant among the nations. Yahweh is the speaking voice in vv. 2–3; in the remaining verses it is Micah.

Grand prophecies of hope for Israel and the world—a reunited Israel under a Davidic king; an end to war, bringing peace, security, and plenty; a return of exiles scattered abroad; and a salvation having worldwide dimensions—all of which develops into later messianism—did not begin during the years of Babylonian exile (Ezek 34:11—48:35; Isa 40–55), nor during Josiah's early reign or the decade before Jerusalem's destruction (Jer 23:5–8; 29:1—33:26), but much earlier. They are present in Hosea, Micah, and Isaiah and rooted earlier in the Song of Moses, which is dated to circa 900 BC (Deut 32:1–43). Isaiah sees the future as a return to the idyllic garden of Eden (Isa 11:1–9). As Hermann Gunkel put it, "Endzeit gleicht Urzeit." End Times will be like Beginning Times.

A RULER TO COME FROM BETHLEHEM (MIC 5:2–6)

Yahweh begins by addressing Bethlehem in the district of Ephrathah, saying he will bring forth from it one who is to be ruler in Israel. Ephrathah was inhabited by a Judahite clan of the same name (Gen 35:16, 19; 48:7)—an extended clan of David from Bethlehem (1 Sam 17:12; Ruth 1:2; 4:11). The clan was small; nevertheless, Yahweh had chosen from it Israel's future king (1 Sam 16). Something similar occurred in the choice of Gideon and Saul. Gideon, when called by Yahweh to deliver Israel from the Midianites, responded, "How can I deliver Israel? My clan is the weakest in Manasseh, and I am the least in my family" (Judg 6:15). When Saul was chosen to be king, he said to Samuel, "I am only a Benjaminite, from the least of the tribes of Israel, and my family is the humblest of all the families of the tribe of Benjamin" (1 Sam 9:21).

With Yahweh promising to raise up a future king the likes of David, one cannot help but wonder if this might not have been an implicit rejection of Judah's current king? According to the Deuteronomic Historian Ahaz was a bad king (2 Kgs 16:2–4); Isaiah had no success prophesying to him, deciding finally to roll up his teaching, retire from public life, and wait for Yahweh, in whom alone was hope (Isa 8:16–17). Isaiah reemerged in the reign of Hezekiah. The present prophecy could therefore have been spoken in the time of Ahaz and originally fulfilled in Hezekiah (cf. 2 Kgs 18:3). Hezekiah was in the Davidic royal line (Matt 1:9). Ancient origins of this future king again point to someone the likes of David (Amos 9:11; cf. Jer 23:5–6 [33:14–16]; Ezek 34:20–31; 37:15–28). Israel was anxiously awaiting him and the deliverance he will bring, like a woman in labor waiting to bear her child (cf. Isa 7:14). For other prophecies of a future king the likes of David, see Hos 3:5; Isa 9:2–7; 11:1–9; 16:5; and 30:8–9. These prophecies build on the eternal covenant sworn to David in 2 Sam 7, echoed also in Pss 89 and 132.

ON THE REMNANT OF JACOB (MIC 5:7–9)

Yahweh then speaks of a remnant of his kin returning to the children of Israel, mentioned again in v. 7. Talk of a remnant began in earnest with Micah and Isaiah (Mic 2:12; 4:6–7; 5:3, 7–8; 7:18; Isa 7:3; 10:20–22; 11:11, 16; 28:5), with Isaiah naming one of his sons Shear-jashub, "A Remnant Will Return" (Isa 7:3). Amos said there may be a "remnant of Joseph" (Amos 5:15), which would refer to those exiled to Assyria in 734 BC and any who might survive final destruction of the north, but one wonders if he really believed it.

In Micah's and Isaiah's prophecies spoken before Sennacherib's campaign into Judah, the remnant would be Israelites exiled to Assyria. Assyrian kings carried away Israelites after overrunning Galilee and Transjordan in 734 (2 Kgs 15:29), and more after destroying Samaria in 722 (2 Kgs 17:6, 23; cf. 18:11). When Sennacherib ravaged Judah in the years prior to 701, taking forty-six fortified cities and many smaller villages, the Bible records nothing about Judahites being carried off (2 Kgs 18:13), but the Assyrian king does in his annals. He says people driven out of Judah's cities were handed over to the kings of Ashdod, Ekron, and Gaza (*ANET*³, 288). Should the date of any prophecy be from this time, exiled Judahites would have to be included in the remnant. But Isaiah talking to Hezekiah about a remnant is referring to Judahites remaining in Jerusalem in the 701 siege (2 Kgs 19:4 [Isa 37:4]; 2 Kgs 19:30–31 [Isa 37:31–32]).

The prophet becomes speaker in v. 4. The future king will stand and rule (literally "tend the flock") in the strength of Yahweh and in the majestic name of Yahweh. He will feed his flock and make them dwell securely as a good shepherd would. The king will be the shepherd-king like David (Jer 23:1–6; Ezek 34). Like David he will be great "to the ends of the earth" (5:4; Zech 9:10; Ps 2:8). His dominion will be universal. Peace and security will reign, for he will be the "One of Peace" (5:5).

Assyria will indeed come into the land and tread in its cities, as in fact it did, but the prophet is confident that Assyria will be overcome. Israel will raise up "seven shepherds and eight princes" (5:5), referring to leaders who will overcome the menace and rule Assyria with the sword. The numerical "seven . . . eight" progression indicates an indefinite number (Prov 30:15, 18, 21, 29; Eccl 11:2; Amos 1:3, 6, 9, 11, 13; etc.). Nimrod was a legendary figure from hoary antiquity, said to be the builder of Babylon and Assyria (5:6; Gen 10:8–12).

The second prophecy (5:7–9) describes the triumph of Israel's remnant. It will dominate amid many peoples and be like dew from Yahweh and showers upon grass. It will not wait for anyone; its fate will be in the hands of God (5:7). The remnant is compared to a lion and other nations to defenseless sheep in the face of Yahweh's strength (5:8; 4:11–13). The prophet concludes by saying that all of Yahweh's enemies will be cut off (5:9; cf. Deut 32:34–43).

REFLECTION

1. How was Mic 5:1–9 later interpreted in the New Testament? See Matt 2:6.

2. What has the "remnant of Jacob" become today? See Rom 9–11.

3. Was this and other messianic texts of the Old Testament completely fulfilled in Jesus, or is there more fulfillment to come? Wars are still with us, and peace comes and goes.

4. How do the Messianic texts tie in with the grand vision given in Rev 12–22?

16

"WHAT DOES YAHWEH REQUIRE OF YOU?" (MIC 6:1-8)

6 ¹*Hear now what Yahweh is saying:*
Up, make your case before the mountains
and let the hills hear your voice
²*Hear you mountains the case of Yahweh*
and you enduring foundations of the earth
For Yahweh has a case with his people
and with Israel he will argue:
³*"My people, what have I done to you*
or in what way have I wearied you? Answer me!
⁴*For I brought you up from the land of Egypt*
and from the house of slavery I redeemed you
And I sent before you Moses
Aaron and Miriam
⁵*My people, remember now what he devised*
Balak king of Moab
and what Balaam son of Beor answered him

From Shittim to Gilgal
in order to know the righteous acts of Yahweh."
6*With what shall I come to meet Yahweh*
I bow myself to God on high?
Shall I come to meet him with burnt offerings
with calves a year old?
7*Will Yahweh be delighted with thousands of rams*
with ten thousands of rivers of oil?
Shall I give my firstborn for my transgression
the fruit of my body for the sin of my soul?
8*He told you O man what is good*
and what Yahweh requires from you
But to do justice and love steadfastness
and walk humbly with your God.

THESE VERSES FORM A self-contained unit, delimited as they are at both ends by section markings in the Hebrew Bible. Three speakers are carrying on a dialogue: Micah is speaking in vv. 1–2; Yahweh is speaking in vv. 3–5; the people are speaking in vv. 6–7; and Micah is speaking again in v. 8. This passage is one for which Micah is known, stating what Yahweh requires of his people.

HEAR NOW WHAT YAHWEH IS SAYING (MIC 6:1–8)

After an opening call by the prophet to hear what Yahweh is saying (cf. 1:2), Micah tells the people to make their case before the mountains and hills that will act as witnesses (6:1–2; cf. Deut 32:1). The mountains and foundations of the earth are also called to witness the case Yahweh has against the people. This is apostrophe; nevertheless, the enduring works of creation have been around from time immemorial, and will be there for a long time to come, making them eminently suitable as witnesses, more so than any human, whose life on earth is but a breath (Job 7:7, 16; Ps 39:5, 11; 144:3–4). This is a lawsuit, and Micah is inviting both people and Yahweh to make their cases. The disputation style is drawn from judicial proceedings in the city gate, occurring also in Amos, Hosea, and other prophets (Amos 7:4; Hos 2:2; 4:1, 4; 12:2; Isa 3:13–14; Jer 2:5–9; 25:31).

The people have no case to make, but Yahweh has one. Yahweh begins by asking his people what he has done to them. In what way has he wearied them? From their silence Yahweh demands an answer! Yahweh redeemed them from Egyptian slavery. He sent before them Moses, Aaron, and Miriam. Other redemptive acts were carried out. People should also remember how Balak, king of Moab, called Balaam to curse Israel, and what Balaam had to tell him (Num 22–24). The curse was turned into a blessing (Deut 23:5; Josh 24:9–10; Neh 13:2). A recently discovered text at Deir 'Allā in Jordan, dated circa 700 BC, mentions Balaam the seer. Micah has a positive remembrance of Balaam, who elsewhere in tradition was either censured or discredited. Balaam was implicated in the romp Israel had with Baal of Peor and the daughters of Moab after the settlement in Transjordan (Num 31:16; cf. Rev 2:14), which explains why Moses and the Israelites killed him along with the kings of Midian (Num 31:8). Balaam was censured for practicing divination (Josh 13:22), and was later reckoned to be a false prophet. A Dead Sea Scroll fragment (4Q339) has turned up listing eight false prophets who arose in Israel, and on the list is Balaam [son of] Beor.

"From Shittim to Gilgal" (Mic 6:5) refers to the crossing of the Jordan River, where Shittim was the last camping-station in Moab, and Gilgal where Israel first arrived west of the Jordan (Josh 2–4). Here again, Shittim and Gilgal otherwise have negative associations in the minds of the prophets. Shittim is where Israel had its sexual romp with Baal of Peor and the daughters of Moab (Num 25; cf. Hos 5:2), and Gilgal where more recent things displeasing to Yahweh have taken place (Amos 4:4; 5:5; Hos 4:15; 12:11). Hosea said it was at Gilgal that Yahweh began to hate his people (Hos 9:15), which is pretty strong. But Micah is remembering Yahweh's righteous or saving acts.

The people become the speaking voice. They had no case to make, but now want to know how they should come to meet their God and bow down before him. Shall they come with whole burnt offerings and yearling calves having a greater value? (6:6) Yearling calves were prescribed for certain sin offerings (Lev 9:2–3). Priests would doubtless be asking for these. Would Yahweh be delighted with thousands of rams and ten thousands of rivers of oil (6:7)? Isaiah had an answer for this (Isa 1:11). Grain offerings were made with oil (Lev 2:1–15; 9:4), and priests would also be delighted with these. At the dedication of the temple Solomon is said to have offered two thousand oxen and twenty thousand sheep (1 Kgs 8:63). Is Yahweh asking for the sacrifice of a firstborn to atone for one's sin? Kings and ordinary people were doing this in Micah's time and even after (2 Kgs 16:3; 17:17; 21:6; Jer 7:31; 19:4–5), and should not have been, for Yahweh put an end to child sacrifice once and for all on Mount Moriah (Gen 22:1–19; Lev 18:21).

The prophet then provides people with an answer. Yahweh has told each and every one of them what is good, and what he requires. It is to do justice, love steadfastness, and walk humbly with their God (6:8). This is a signature statement of Micah's, but it has echoes in other prophets. In the Talmud it is said to be "a quintessence of the 613 commandments of the Bible" (*Makkot* 24a). On justice, see Mic 3:1, 8–9; Amos 5:7, 15, 24; 6:12; Hos 2:19; 12:6; Isa 1:17; 5:7;

Hab 1:4, 7; Jer 4:2; 5:1, 28; etc. Steadfastness is what binds Yahweh and people together in covenant love (Deut 7:9, 12; Ps 89:49), and Micah says Yahweh delights in it, having shown it to Abraham in former days (7:18, 20). Isaiah says Yahweh expects justice, not bloodshed (Isa 1:15–17; 5:7). "Steadfastness" (*ḥesed*) was a favorite term of Hosea (Hos 2:19; 4:1; 6:4, 6; 10:12; 12:6; cf. Jer 2:2), and in the present verse is better than the KJV's "mercy," which has been retained in the NIV.

REFLECTION

1. Does God have a case against people today who are confident about having been saved by the blood of Jesus?

2. What saving acts of God—ancient and more recent—have been influential in your life?

3. At my home church, Mic 6:8 is inscribed on the back side of the signboard for people to see as they leave the church building. Is it a good reminder after one has attended a service of worship?

4. In my town today, many people have signs on their lawns saying JUSTICE NOW. Could this be God speaking to us?

17

"THE VOICE OF YAHWEH
CALLS TO THE CITY"
(MIC 6:9-16)

6 9The voice of Yahweh calls to the city
 and wisdom perceives your name
  Hear O tribe, so who can arraign it?
10Is there still a house of the wicked
 stores of wickedness
  and a cursed scant ephah?
11Shall I make clean with scales of wickedness
 and with a bag of wrong weights?
12When its rich are full of violence
 and its inhabitants speak lies
  and their tongue is deceit in their mouth?
13As for me, I am indeed sick of smiting you
 of devastating on account of your sins
14You, you shall eat, but not be satisfied
 and I will make you empty in your inner parts

And you will carry away but will not save
   and what you do save I will give over to the sword
15 You, you shall sow but not harvest
   you, you shall tread olives but not anoint yourself with
   oil
      as for new wine, you will not drink wine
16 Yes, you have kept the statutes of Omri
   and all the doings of the house of Ahab
   and have walked in their counsels
In order that I make you a desolation
   and her inhabitants an object of hissing
      and the reproach of my people you shall bear.

THE VOICE OF YAHWEH CALLS (MIC 6:9)

THE PRESENT VERSES ARE a unit, being delimited at both ends by section markings in the Hebrew Bible. The opening "Hear" (6:9) appears also in 3:1, 9; and 6:1. In the present v. 9 the prophet is introducing a word from Yahweh to the city of Jerusalem and the tribe of Judah. The remaining verses (vv. 10–16) are Yahweh's indictment and judgment on Judah and Jerusalem. The voice of Yahweh is calling the city to account. The next colon ("and wisdom perceives your name") is obscure. Is Micah referring to the name of Jerusalem, the city of peace (cf. Ps 122:6–7)? The third colon ("Hear O tribe, so who can arraign it?") is a rhetorical question. Micah asks his southern tribe who is able to summon its capital city to court. Answer: Yahweh.

SCANT EPHAHS, WICKED SCALES, AND WRONG WEIGHTS (MIC 6:10–16)

Yahweh is now the speaking voice, asking if there is still a house of the wicked, stores of wickedness, and the cursed ephah that is less than it should be (v. 10). This is about weights and measures, and a strong word to merchants who are accumulating wealth by cheating in the marketplace and in houses. Measuring grain could also take place in houses (6:10). The ephah was a dry measure equal to three-fifths of a bushel. Grain was commonly measured by the ephah. The corresponding liquid measure was the bath (Isa 5:10). Deuteronomy says, "There shall not be for you in your house one ephah and another ephah, great and small" (Deut 25:14; cf. Lev 19:35–36). Fraudulent measuring practices were widespread in antiquity, for which reason prophets railed against them. Amos scored merchants trampling the needy and bringing ruin to the poor by selling grain in small ephahs. He also found that merchants were the biggest grumblers about sabbath and holiday closures (Amos 8:4–5). Greed is the handmaiden of social injustice. Dishonest practices continued in the time of Ezekiel, who told princes to put away violence and oppression and have an honest ephah and an honest bath (Ezek 45:10).

The other problem was false scales and weights, and Yahweh asks how he can declare Jerusalem clean when it has scales of wickedness and bags with wrong weights (Mic 6:11). In preexilic Israel, traders and merchants carried with them a pair of scales suspended from a bar (Zeph 1:11). They also had a bag of stone weights inscribed with numbers and symbols for a shekel or fraction of a shekel. Excavations have turned up weights from Micah's time at Lachish, which is just south of the prophet's hometown of Moresheth. Weights commonly came in sets so that fine differences could be weighed out. On one scale the merchant placed his stones, which were shaped like round loaves of bread, and on the other scale were placed the goods to be bought or sold. The problem was, some merchants had in their bags different weights marked with the same denominations—one set for purchasing and another for selling. That is how they got rich. Once again, Deuteronomy mandated full and right stones if Israel hoped to live long in the land (Deut 25:13–15; cf. Lev 19:35–36). Prophets, too, spoke about honest weights and balances, decrying their lack in the marketplace (Hos 12:7; Mic 6:11; Ezek 25:10). In the book of Proverbs false balances, weights, and measures are said to be an abomination to Yahweh (Prov 11:1; 20:10, 23). Yahweh now asks how he can declare the city clean when traders and merchants are full of violence, speaking lies, and making fraudulent claims with the tongues in their mouth.

Yahweh will now pronounce judgment on those summoned in Mic 6:9 and indicted in 6:10–12. Yahweh says he is sick of smiting and devastating on account of people's sins (cf. Amos 4:6–11). Nevertheless, he speaks "futility curses" (Mic 6:14–15) like those appearing in the ancient Near Eastern treaties, found also in Deuteronomy (Deut 28:30–31, 38–41), and echoed in other prophets (Hos 4:10; 8:7; Amos 5:11). People will eat, but not be satisfied (Lev 26:26), for Yahweh will make their insides empty; they will carry away what they can, but not be able to save it. Anything they do manage to save will be given over to the sword, which may mean they will die with it in hand. In Hosea the curse is a loss of cherished offspring after birth or after the parents have brought them up (Hos 9:12, 16). Farmers will sow seed but not harvest a crop; they will tread olives but not be able to rub themselves with oil. As for new wine, they will not drink any wine.

Yahweh shames the wicked merchants of Jerusalem by saying that they have walked in the statutes of two of North Israel's evil kings, Omri and Ahab (Mic 6:16a; cf. 2 Kgs 17:19). The Deuteronomic History has nothing good to say about either, who walked in the sins of an even worse king, Jeroboam I (1 Kgs 16:21–22:40).

Finally Yahweh says all this is happening in order to make Judah and Jerusalem a desolation, hissed at by an enemy (Mic 6:16b; Jer 25:9; 51:37), suffering even more by having to bear reproach from Yahweh's people who one day will realize that things went terribly wrong. This prophecy could allude to Sennacherib's destruction of Judah in 701 BC and its aftermath.

REFLECTION

1. What are some ways buyers and sellers today take advantage of people to become rich?

2. Do Better Business Bureaus and Consumer Advocacy Groups help in our society?

3. Does Micah's prophecy tie in with any of Jesus's New Testament teachings? Do you see God coming to judge cheaters and other dishonest people in this life or the next?

4. Do the ways of our president and other leaders have an effect on the way more ordinary people do things?

BIBLIOGRAPHY

Bright, John. *A History of Israel*. 3rd ed. Westminster Aids to the Study of Scripture. Philadelphia: Westminster, 1981.

Cathcart, Kevin J., and Robert P. Gordon, trans. *The Targum of the Minor Prophets*. ArBib 14. Wilmington, DE: Glazier, 1989.

Chadwick, Jeffrey R., and Aren M. Maeir. "Judahite Gath in the Eighth Century BCE." *NEA* 81 (2018) 48–54.

Chaney, Marvin L. *Peasants, Prophets, and Political Economy: The Hebrew Bible and Social Analysis*. Eugene, OR: Cascade Books, 2017.

Cheyne, T. K. *Hosea*. CBSC. Cambridge: Cambridge University Press, 1887.

Driver, S. R. *The Books of Joel and Amos*. CBSC. Cambridge: Cambridge University Press, 1901.

Eissfeldt, Otto. *The Old Testament: An Introduction*. Translated by Peter R. Ackroyd; New York: Harper & Row, 1965.

Gunkel, Hermann. "Israelite Prophecy from the Time of Amos." In *Twentieth Century Theology in the Making*, edited by Jaroslav Pelikan, 1:48–75. 3 vols. Translated by R. A. Wilson. New York: Harper & Row, 1969 (German original 1930).

Heschel, Abraham Joshua. *The Prophets*. New York: Harper & Row, 1962.

Hillers, Delbert R. *Micah*. Hermeneia. Philadelphia: Fortress, 1984.

King, Philip J. "Amos." In *JBC*, edited by Raymond E. Brown et al., 245–52. 2 vols. Englewood Cliffs, NJ: Prentice-Hall, 1968.

———. *Amos, Hosea, Micah: An Archaeological Commentary*. Philadelphia: Westminster, 1988.

———. "Micah." In *JBC*, edited by Raymond E. Brown et al., 283–89. 2 vols. Englewood Cliffs, NJ: Prentice-Hall, 1968.

Luker, Lamontte M. "Moresheth." In *ABD* 4:904.

Bibliography

Lundbom, Jack R. *Biblical Rhetoric and Rhetorical Criticism*. Hebrew Bible Monographs 45. Sheffield: Sheffield Phoenix, 2013.

————. "Contentious Priests and Contentious People in Hosea 4:1–10." *VT* 36 (1986) 52–70. Reprinted in Lundbom, *Biblical Rhetoric and Rhetorical Criticism*, 216–31.

————. "Delimitation of Units in the Book of Jeremiah." In *The Impact of Unit Delimitation on Exegesis*, edited by Raymond de Hoop et al., 146–74. Pericope 7. Leiden: Brill, 2009. Reprinted in Lundbom, *Biblical Rhetoric and Rhetorical Criticism*, 37–59.

————. *Deuteronomy: A Commentary*. Grand Rapids; Eerdmans, 2013.

————. *The Hebrew Prophets: An Introduction*. Minneapolis: Fortress, 2010.

————. "The Lion Has Roared: Rhetorical Structure in Amos 1:2—3:8." In *Milk and Honey: Essays on Ancient Israel and the Bible in Appreciation of the Judaic Studies Program at the University of California, San Diego*, edited by Sarah Malena and David Miano, 65–75. Winona Lake, IN: Eisenbrauns, 2007. Reprinted in Lundbom, *Biblical Rhetoric and Rhetorical Criticism*, 202–12.

————. "Poetic Structure and Prophetic Rhetoric in Hosea." *VT* 29 (1979) 300–308. Reprinted in *Prophecy in the Hebrew Bible: Selected Studies from "Vetus Testamentum,"* compiled by David E. Orton, 139–47. Brill's Readers in Biblical Studies 5. Leiden: Brill, 2000. Also reprinted in Lundbom, *Biblical Rhetoric and Rhetorical Criticism*, 232–39.

————. "Prophets in the Hebrew Bible." In *The Oxford Research Encyclopedia of Religion*, edited by John Barton. New York: Oxford University Press, 2016. http://religion.oxfordre. com.

Luther, Martin. *Lectures on the Minor Prophets I*. Edited by Hilton C. Oswald. Luther's Works 18. St. Louis: Concordia, 1975.

Maeir, Aren M. "The Tell eṣ-Ṣâfi / Gath Archaeological Project: Overview." *NEA* 80 (2017) 212–31.

McCarthy Dennis J. "Hosea." In *JBC*, edited by Raymond E. Brown et al., 1:253–64. 2 vols. Englewood Cliffs, NJ: Prentice-Hall, 1968.

Muilenburg, James. "Old Testament Prophecy." In *Peake's Commentary on the Bible*, edited by Mathew Black and H. H. Rowley, 475–83. London: Nelson, 1977.

Paul, Shalom. *Amos*. Hermeneia. Minneapolis: Fortress, 1991.

Rad, Gerhard von. "The Origin of the Concept of the Day of Yahweh." *JSS* 4 (1959) 97–108.

Robinson, H. Wheeler. "Prophetic Symbolism." In *Old Testament Essays*, edited by D. C. Simpson, 1–17. London: Griffin, 1927.

Bibliography

Wellhausen, Julius. *Die kleinen Propheten übersetz und erklärt.* 3rd ed. Berlin: Reimer, 1898. Originally 1892.

Wolff, Hans Walter. *Hosea.* Translated by Gary Stansell. Hermeneia. Philadelphia: Fortress, 1974. German original, 1965.

———. *Joel and Amos.* Translated by Waldemar Janzen et al. Hermeneia. Philadelphia: Fortress, 1977.

AUTHOR INDEX

SCRIPTURE INDEX

✧